INTRODUCING YOUR KIDS TO THE OUTDOORS

INTRODUCING YOUR KIDS

(Revised Edition)

Distributed by

**Stackpole Books
Cameron and Kelker Streets
Harrisburg, PA 17105**

TO THE OUTDOORS

by
Joan Dorsey

Published by

Stone Wall Press, Inc.
1241 30th Street, N.W.
Washington, D.C. 20007

First Printing—March, 1978   ISBN 0-913276-34-0
Second Edition—March, 1982

Contents

Dedication

To Karen and Ellen, and especially to Jack.

Acknowledgement

Jack Dorsey, Dolly Czupryna and Henry Wheelwright have all helped me in planning and preparing this book, and I'm grateful for the time and work they've given me.

I also want to thank all my friends, especially Ann Fontaine and Judy Curtis, for their encouragement. A special thanks, also, to Faith Wilkinson for providing me with some photographs.

Preface to Second Edition

Since INTRODUCING YOUR KIDS TO THE OUTDOORS was first printed three years ago, many new products have made life for the camping family even more fun than it was then! This second edition includes some details about these new developments.

The second edition also allows me to present material and ideas from a new perspective. My children are now eight and nine-years-old; we have, therefore, moved into a new era of family life outdoors. Rather than wistfully guessing what it would be like to take a family bike tour, I can now share such joys with you first-hand.

Since 1978 I know I have made some converts. I've seen more families out in the woods, and I've heard from a number of people who are now enjoying the wilderness with their children. My greatest hope is that, with this new volume, more people will enjoy the outdoors with their young children.

Introduction

In a world of nuclear threats and rising crime rates, something very positive and encouraging has happened: more and more people are turning to physical activity and wilderness encounters to enrich their lives. Several years ago wild areas were almost exclusively for fishing and macho-ego trips. Occasionally a woman would venture into the wilderness. Now canoeing, backpacking, ski-touring and bicycling have been steadily gaining in popularity. Young people and old, men and women, all have been experimenting with these outdoor pursuits and like them. Doctors have found that regular physical activity can help reduce tension as well as strengthen muscles and vital organs. Those who choose the active way of life not only enrich, but probably lengthen their lives as well.

Unfortunately there is one group that is usually excluded from this movement: children. While mom and dad are out developing cardio-vascular fitness by jogging around town, the child is apt to be sitting on the bench at a little league game. And while the parents are hiking above tree line, the kids are likely to be watching Saturday morning television with a babysitter. The result? Another generation which regards "sport" as something that requires two teams of at least five people. A generation that views the wilderness as the backdrop for a Yogi Bear cartoon.

What do you do if you are an outdoor enthusiast and all of a sudden have a baby on your hands? There are several options. You can stay home until your child grows up; you can get a baby-sitter or send your son or daughter to Grandma's, and go camping; or, you can take the whole family and head for the woods. That's what my family has done. We have found an experience that draws us closer both to nature and to each other—and is fun, satisfying, and educational.

In choosing your option, ask yourself what you want for your child's future. Do you want him to actively enjoy this side of life that you have discovered? Or, do you want him to be one of life's spectators, watching others play tennis or baseball on television from an armchair? Do you want him to discover the wilderness just by reading Thoreau, or by listening to tales people like yourself bring back from the woods? Do you want him to learn it firsthand? If you want your boy or girl to enjoy the good life as you know it, you have a responsibility to introduce your child to it when he's young. And, if you want him for your wilderness companion as a youth, your best bet is to introduce him to it at as young an age as possible.

If you take your baby or toddler on one wilderness outing, chances are you'll be eager to go again. It's great fun, and just made for the uninhibited ways of young children. Children were made for the natural life; they thrive on it. And there are lessons in the woods and in the interdependent life of camping that most modern children have no other opportunity to learn. Fussy appetites, television, and toy "addictions" tend to disappear. Sharing becomes an essential part of life, as does ecological and environmental awareness.

Young children can thrive in today's wilderness just as safely, comfortably, and happily as pioneer children once did. You may need some special equipment and make some modifications in your plans. But you'll certainly get some compensation for your efforts and inconvenience. By introducing your kids to the outdoors, you will find a special closeness—away from the distractions of home duties, work, school activities and playmates. By encouraging your child to turn toward wilderness sports, you can fuel interests that can lead to a healthy, wholesome life. By developing a concern for wilderness in this next generation, you can promote its protection in lifetimes still to come.

My aim in writing this book is to show that exploring the wilderness with very young children is both possible and fun. I'd like to share a few of the pointers that I've learned, sometimes the hard way, in my experiences camping with our two young daughters. Yes, that's right—daughters. The wilderness is not a place just for the annual father-and-son outing; it's for the whole family. We noticed when cross-country skiing this winter with our daughters, that everyone we met thought they must be boys. "How old is he?" we would be asked. It was assumed that only little boys would be out roughing it. No, I don't expect them to grow up to be a couple of Amazons. At 102 pounds, I'm hardly muscle-bound myself (even though I often wish I were a little more so), but I've been able to keep up with any group in which I've travelled. I see nothing feminine or masculine about outdoor activities. They are simply a pleasurable way of life for anyone who is reasonably fit.

We've taken our children on day trips of all sorts: hiking, bicycling, ski touring and canoeing. Our wilderness camping trips are mainly involved with canoeing, and our children have been along since they were as young as six weeks old. While this may seem extreme, I have always been completely satisfied that, with my husband's and my own experience, the precautions we have taken, and the advance preparations we have made, our children were never in danger. In fact, I'm convinced that the most dangerous part of the trips we've taken is the automobile ride to the wilderness starting point. An article entitled *"Can Safety be Legislated"* by Carl Trost in *Down River* compared casualty rates of automobile and canoe mishaps, basing the study on statistics from the National Safety Council and the Coast Guard. They found that the risks involved in a six-hour canoe trip are comparable to travelling 100 miles in an automobile.

If you're new to the wilderness yourself, don't worry about trying it as a family. Two major obstacles keep people from trying the wilderness experience. The first is the myth that the only people suited for wilderness camping are a combination of the old voyageurs, Thoreau's Joe Attean and Sacajawea. We've run into people on our trips who fit these images. We've also run into people who fit every image from that of Shirley Temple to Grandma Moses. All were doing perfectly fine. The secret is that you must gear the trip to your ability and needs, not the movie producer's picture of the ultimate wilderness test. You're not out to test yourself; you're out to have a good time.

The second factor that keeps people from trying wilderness camping is that they don't make time for it. There are always responsibilities, things to do around the house, all sorts of chores cropping up which keep folks saying "Well, next year..." The trouble is that "next year" never comes. So, many would-be wilderness families spend their vacations painting the house or shopping for back-to-school clothes. MAKE time for it. Chances are the house painting could be postponed another year. If you wait until mid-September to buy the school clothes, they might even be on sale. Don't forget that your children don't wait to grow up. If you put it off too long, you will have missed the opportunity altogether.

There's a bright note to keep in mind. Economically speaking, a vacation in the wilderness will probably cost less than most any other way you might spend your time, including fixing up the house. A few years ago we figured it all out and discovered it cost us less to go on vacation for two weeks than it cost us to stay home. Sure, we used a considerable amount of gas to get from our house to northern Maine where our trip started, but once we arrived, the car sat unused for two weeks. Our food costs were about the same, maybe slightly higher. And, of course, we were not using electricity, or the telephone, or making trips to the store for magazines and little goodies which tend to add up to a bit of money.

How do you get started? My first camping experience was a four-week honeymoon spent camping in Canada. Luckily, I liked camping from the start, but looking back on it, the trip could have proved a shock treatment, discouraging me about future wilderness trips. I suggest starting small and starting short. Take a few day trips in the beginning or, if you are bringing toddlers on their first excursions, you may want to start with half-day trips. After you get used to things a bit, you can progress to an overnight trip, a long weekend, then graduate to an extended camping trip of a week or longer.

Make it easy. Your children will probably have much more fun if they can easily accomplish what you have set out to do. If you want to climb a mountain, find one with a fairly short and gradual trail. If you start out canoeing, try to avoid making your first day trip one which requires six or seven portages. Don't take your little ones skiing for the first time when the snow is crusted with ice. I always try to keep in mind that old adage about first impressions.

Make it fun. Set an interesting goal for each trip. I've found my girls can hike a long way if it leads to a mountain overlook from which they can see clear to Boston. Or to a bunch of wild blueberry bushes loaded with ripe berries. They can ski farther if the trail leads to a place where horses are kept. Even on a rather monotonous lake crossing, they will stay interested if we look and listen for different kinds of birds, or sing songs together as we paddle across. To an older child becoming bored on a long backpacking trip, a day spent trying to forage for food can be an

5

interesting break from the routine, and something to tell his friends about when he gets home. And, speaking of friends, a good way to maintain an older child's interest in the family camping trip is, if practical, to allow him to bring along a friend from home.

In her book on child fitness, Suzy Prudden says, *"Parents and children may follow one of two roads. One choice leads to health, creativity and happiness; the other choice merely ends in sloth and softness."** I've made my choice and I hope that you'll give this *"road"* a try, too. It's worth at least a try, because it can make a world of difference to you personally, to the future of your child, and to your happiness as a family.

---

*Prudden, *Creative Fitness For Baby and Child*, Prentice-Hall, page 75.

1. THE DAY TRIP

The easiest way for your family to begin exploring the outdoors is to start with a short day trip and build gradually toward
longer camping trips. Day trips are very pleasant diversions. They
are not only the starting point for your family's adventures in the
wilderness, this kind of trip will provide you with many bright
weekends around your home territory. Should you find yourselves
travelling as tourists in another part of the country, or another part
of the world, a short day trip into the surrounding wilderness can
give you a better feel for that environ than any number of guided
tours, and can be a great source of relaxation.

No matter where you live, even in the most industrialized and
developed areas, a short hike in the woods, an afternoon's paddle on a little stream or lake, a ski tour across a country club's golf
course and surrounding land, or a bike ride along the roads of a
state forest is probably only a short distance away. And there's
no better way to relax than to literally "get away from it all," leave
your house chores and business worries behind, pack your lunch
and a few belongings, and start looking for places to explore.

Very little expertise and very little equipment is necessary. If
you decide to try canoeing, bicycling, or ski touring, you can rent

the equipment you will need. For day hiking, all you really need is a good pair of shoes. While good sneakers or a comfortable pair of shoes will suffice for very short, easy hikes, you may want to invest in a pair of hiking boots. A good hiking boot is a good investment. Though rather expensive, they last so long that they are well worth the price. My husband still wears the same pair of boots he had custom-made in a North Conway, New Hampshire shop fifteen years ago! They are not only old, they have had a **LOT** of use. They may not look beautiful, but neither do my comparatively new ones after a day of walking along muddy trails.

For the children, hiking boots can be purchased for anyone big enough to walk, if you look hard enough. And there is an added bonus—they make great beginner ski boots when coupled with a pair of cable bindings on a little pair of cross-country skis. We generally buy each child a pair of boots in late fall, fitting them with a size large enough to wear over heavy wool socks. They're great for playing in the muddy fall ground. When the snow falls, they become ski boots. By spring they are getting to be about the right size to be worn over socks of regular weight, so they are the play shoes in which my daughters are seen most frequently. Then, by the time our summer camping trips are over, the shoes have fulfilled their many purposes and proven themselves well worth the money we paid (little more than the price of an ordinary pair of children's shoes). By then we are ready to re-equip. The little boots may not be as pretty as their patent leather Mary Janes, but they sure get worn a lot more often!

Whether you're travelling by bike, canoe, ski, or foot, one piece of equipment is indispensable for day tripping and very versatile: The Day Pack. A good day pack, which costs under twenty dollars even for a relatively sophisticated model, is a useful necessity. It frees your hands for holding other hands, and it's a comfortable way to carry the gear you'll need for the day. If you check your nearest wilderness equipment store or mail order catalogue, you'll find a variety of models made by well-known manufacturers as well as some you've never heard of before. There are two basic shapes—the typical rucksack design, which is simply a sack-type arrangement with shoulder

Standard Day Pack

Teardrop Day Pack

Child's Pack

straps, and the teardrop pack named for its characteristic shape. Many people find the teardrop pack more comfortable. Some are made of simple duck or rip-stop nylon, others are fashioned of coated fabric to keep the contents dry. If you choose an un-coated pack, you can always waterproof your belongings by putting a plastic garbage bag inside the pack and closing the top of it tightly with a rubber band.

Just which pack you will pick will depend a great deal upon personal preference and also on the amount of cash on hand. Don't be afraid to buy an inexpensive model, as long as it meets certain standards. The shoulder straps should be spaced closely enough together so that the pack can be comfortably worn. This is the most frequent shortcoming of many discount store and box-top knapsacks. The straps themselves should have a bit of padding around the shoulders for comfort. Another feature which makes a pack more pleasant to wear is a waist band to secure the pack to the body. This keeps the weight you're carrying from shifting position, allowing you to move about more freely. So, find a pack and try it on to test for comfort and also for maneu-verability. Buy the pack which suits you and your pocketbook best. You won't need one for each member of the family—one per family should suffice for day trips, but this pack is not meant to take the place of larger packs used for extended trips.

If you have a toddler or older child, you may also want to invest in a child-size rucksack, because kids usually want to be in on the action. Don't pay too much for this one since it will be outgrown before long. Outfitters sell a nice little child's pack for ten dollars, and even some of the most expensive mountaineering stores carry them for around fifteen.

Like the children's boots, this piece of equipment can suit many purposes. It's great for carrying books to school, brown bag lunches, and toys or clothing for sleep-over nights at the homes of friends and relatives.

Belt and "fanny" packs can be nice supplementary packs, especially for carrying small items such as insect repellent and ski waxes that should be readily accessible. But these are a more dubious investment since their limited capacity is not matched by a small price. They cost nearly as much as the regular-sized day pack. Nonetheless, they are handy; so I mention them here in case your outfitting interests are not hampered by economics.

If you're hiking and have a baby along, you'll need a pack for carrying her. The kiddy pack is as commonplace a baby gift nowadays as the play pen or high chair. Nearly every mother has one, even if she has never had any intention of setting foot off the beaten path. This pack is used for carrying children along on all types of activities—shopping trips, spectator sports, you name it. They are also the greatest pacifiers ever invented. My younger daughter spent practically the first three months of her life in one of these packs, when she suffered from cholic. Some psychologists and anthropologists say that cultures where babies are carried on the parents' persons tend to produce less stressful individuals. I don't know about that, but I do know that it's got to be the easiest way to bring them along when you're hiking.

There are several companies that manufacture these kiddy packs. The most popular that I know of is Gerry®, who makes two different packs to suit different sizes. The first is the Cuddler®, an all-cloth sling for the smallest infant, which can be worn either front or back (front is recommended) and provides good support for the baby too young to support his own head. When the baby can hold his head up well, he can graduate from the Cuddler® to the kiddy pack, which is a canvas and tubular aluminum construction of debatable comfort to the parent. The kids love it, though, riding facing front, looking over mother's or dad's shoulder and occasionally amusing themselves by pulling the parent's hair or twisting an ear or two. We've used both of these packs for our kids and were quite satisfied with them, except that the kiddy pack was not as comfortable as we had hoped. Yet it still beat any other method of transporting the children that we knew of. They rode many miles on our backs, while we travelled both by foot and by ski.

Since our children have become ambulatory, I have noticed a new type of kiddy pack on the market. It looks extremely comfortable, and I have questioned several parents who have praised them highly. The *Snugli Baby Carriers*® were designed by some ex-Peace Corps members who copied them from the sling-type packs used by African mothers for carrying their children. It can be worn either front (for infants) or back (for older babies and tired toddlers.) It is made completely of soft material—no frame—and it has a system of releasable tucks and darts to accommodate the smallest baby to the hefty three-year-old. The only drawback I have been able to find associated with this carrier is the price—more than the cost of the two packs in the Gerry system combined. However, since these apparati seem to get passed along from one baby to the next, from one family to another, you may find it well worth the extra money for superior comfort before it wears out.

Clothing is an important consideration in preparing for a day trip. The system of dressing in layers is now the accepted concept in dressing for the outdoors. Your outfit will vary somewhat according to the type of activity in which you will be participating, but will still follow a pretty classic outdoor pattern. My gear consists of turtleneck shirt (to keep the bugs off the neck), loose-fitting jeans, wool socks, boots, chamois shirt, wool shirt, down vest, windbreaker, light weight rain jacket and pants, wool caps, mits and down parka. I don't wear this whole get-up every time I go out. I'm writing this on a hot day in June and, if I decided to go climb Mount Watatic with my family today, I would leave most of the above-mentioned clothing at home in the closet. On a

The Snugli II Baby Carrier®—Note that it can be worn in front for infants, or in back for older babies and tired toddlers.

The BABY BAG® snowsuit is a new idea for winter activities with infants. Made of lightweight, super-warm material, your infant can be kept happy and warm during a wide variety of cold weather conditions and activities. It works with back carriers, strollers, and bike seats and is even water repellent in a light rain. Available from the BABY BAG company, Camden, Maine.

camping trip, even this time of year, I would bring a complete set of these clothes for each of us since weather, especially here in New England, is unpredictable. But for the day trip, one extra layer up or down from that in which you start is about all you will want. And, if you're not going far or for a long time, and if the sky is clear, you may leave the rain paraphernalia at home. The advantage of the layered system of clothing is that it gives you a maximum number of degrees of warmth for the number and weight of garments you tote, because it allows you to combine in different ways the various articles of clothing you have available.

A few particulars—special tips on clothing for different circumstances and activities:

1. For outdoor summer clothing, it is probably wise to avoid the color blue. It may be just an old wives' tale, but it seems to hold true: Insects, especially black flies and mosquitos, are attracted to the color blue. So, while it is hard to find such clothes, since most jeans, work shirts, etc. are primarily available in blue, I think it's worth shopping around a bit to find alternate colors.

2. Straight-leg pants are preferable to bell-bottom or flared pants. You may think I'm paranoid about bugs, but one reason for this point is that those pesty insects will fly right up the loose, flared bottom of a pant leg. And, if you intend to do any bicycling, bell bottoms catch in the gears and chain. If you must wear them when bicycling, catch them up with a rubber band or pin them together so you don't ruin your pants or you or both.

3. If canoeing is your sport, and the water or air is at all cold, make sure you have woolen clothes since wool is one of few insulating materials (*Polar Guard*®, a synthetic, is another) which keeps you warm even when it is wet. Of course I hope you never venture on the waters in cold weather, or when the water is still extremely cold in early spring anyway, with the children. When my husband and I run the fast, exciting rivers of early spring, it is only with the protection of a diver's wet suit. Now, any water in which I feel safe only in a wet suit is no place for a couple of toddlers. They stay at home, or watch from the banks with their baby-sitter—we'll make up for it all by taking them hiking the next day! If you are at all unsure about the temperature of either air or

water, carry along in the boat an extra set of clothes for each individual, in a waterproof bag or other container. Chances of an upset on still water are very remote, but it always pays to be cautious.

4. If one of the members of your expedition is a passenger only, either riding in a kiddy pack or on the child-carrier seat at the rear of your bicycle, be sure to keep in mind that you are expending more energy than the child and that she may need an additional layer of clothing than what you find comfortable for yourself.

Remember that day pack you purchased a few pages ago? Well, in addition to clothing, you'll want to stuff it with a few other goodies you'll need along the way. If you're skiing, you'll need ski wax; if you're biking, some tools. But we'll get into that in later chapters. Some equipment is basic for any type of outing. A first-aid kit is a must even on the shortest afternoon trip. There are several manufacturers who put out pocket-size kits which are pretty good, but you will probably want to add a few items yourself. Or you may want to start from scratch and put one together entirely on your own. A waterproof container is an asset since soggy bandages and bottles with the labels washed off tend to confuse the medics. Inside, some of the items you'll want are adhesive tape, sterile gauze pads, 2″ gauze bandage, a triangular bandage, antiseptic cream, aspirin and bandaids. Two other items I feel much more comfortable having along are a compact sized first-aid manual and a small bottle of syrup of ipecac. In the out-of-doors there are many poisonous plants, and you may be bringing some additional poisons along yourself, so the ipecac is really important to the family which includes a toddler who likes to experiment along this line. Even if yours is not inclined to experiment, who knows when he may decide to start? Unless you're sure you have scheduled your excursion at a different time than the bugs have scheduled theirs, repellent should also be in your pack. I prefer creams or lotions to aerosols myself, partly because of my concern for the ozone layer and also because if the propellant in your can of spray gives out, you are going to provide a great feast for the surrounding insects. When applying repellent to a baby, it is wise to keep it off of his hands.

Most babies tend to put their fingers in their mouths and rub their eyes. The few bites he gets on his hands are probably less bothersome than the burning sensation of having repellent in the eyes or mouth, and definitely safer. The spots that seem most attractive to insects, I've found, are the baby's head, neck and ears, so be sure to offer protection for these areas, including possibly a hat for head protection.

That hat will do double duty, too, because another type of protection is also needed for your little one, and for you, too: Protection from the sun. A hat is good protection for the face in most cases, but a sunscreen should also be applied to facial skin on an extremely bright day or around water, which tends to reflect the sun. On very sensitive individuals and most infants, an opaque sun blocking cream may be necessary. Kids usually like this, since it makes them look like circus clowns. You may like it less, especially if there is a camera bug in your party.

I have mentioned the importance of protection—bug protection, temperature protection, sun protection, injury protection—in this chapter about day trips because I think it's important. And, as you progress to more ambitious day tripping, your knowledge in these areas will be increasingly important. But, back to that first short, easy trip. . . . On your first several outings, I would try to avoid extremes of heat, cold, or the middle of black fly season, especially if you're in a position where you are trying to *sell* a spouse and/or child on the joys of the outdoor life. After you are all more comfortable with the outdoor world, you will adjust to these small annoyances and take them in stride. But for your first few trips, do your best to make them pleasurable in every way you can.

If you have a baby in your party, you will probably be tucking some spare diapers, a bottle, teething crackers and other such goodies in your day pack, or in the small compartment at the bottom of the baby carrier. Be sure not to carry perishable food without refrigeration. A watertight plastic juice container can become a mini-cooler for a baby bottle by putting the bottle in the middle and packing ice around it; then sealing the container. Most of the standard brands of formula can be purchased in nursing bottles with nipples packed along separately. There's no

18

chance of spoilage if the nurser filled with formula is opened just at the time it will be used. Powdered formula, or powdered milk, can be packed in a nursing bottle dry, then reconstituted on the spot with water packed along in a separate container.

Don't forget that the rest of the family will probably want a snack, too. A container of juice or lemonade and a candy bar or granola bar can make a trail break a fun picnic. On a cold day a snack will warm you up and, on a hot day, the drink will help replenish lost fluids.

In your pack you will also want to include a compass, trail map (or road map, if bicycling), and a guidebook if you are using one. Before you leave home, you should learn to use your compass just in case you ever find you need it. It's easy enough to teach yourself—most come with complete and clear directions—or a friend with experience might help you. An excellent book to study on the subject is *Be Expert With Map and Compass* by Bjorn Kjellstrom, published by the American Orienteering Service.

Now that you're all dressed and packed, you have to find someplace to go. Since you'll probably want to start near home, consult some local sources for ideas on places to explore in your area. Your nearby wilderness equipment dealer, if there is one, is probably one of your best sources. Your state and local conservation commissions, and the local chapter of the Audubon Society are also likely leads. If any schools or colleges in your area offer wilderness exploring or survival courses, the instructors may know of some good locations nearby. In consulting these sources, it is important that you be frank in providing information as to the abilities and experience of the members of your party. Ask for areas with well-marked trails, easy gradient and accessibility. As you become more proficient in your outdoor skills, and more confident, you can become more adventuresome. If you are really nervous, especially if you are canoeing or cross-country skiing for the first time, try starting your wilderness adventures with an experienced family or group. Organizations such as the Sierra Club and the Appalachian Mountain Club frequently conduct group outings for beginners. Check around in your neighborhood and you can probably find the company you require for peace of mind your first few times out.

But really, as you're sure to find, the wilderness is not a very scary place. It's peaceful, beautiful, interesting—a great place for quiet talk and for silent reflection. Just keep telling Junior that when he starts hollering for his bottle! But seriously, my children are usually better behaved and more fun to be around when we're off in the woods than at any other time. Maybe it's because they, too, feel fewer stresses when they're away from it all; maybe it's because their dad and I have more time to talk to them and enjoy them without the inevitable distractions around home. For whatever reason, it makes the time we spend together in the wilderness a special time for all of us. And it will be a special time for you, too.

2. THE EXTENDED TRIP

While the extended wilderness trip is quite a bit more complicated than the day trip, I find such trips more rewarding, and well
worth the extra effort they require. The part that takes the most
effort begins before you even leave home—the planning. But
planning your trip can really be enjoyable because it allows you
lots of time to wish, dream, and explore from your armchair during
the weeks or months before your trip. Most of all, the planning
stage is probably the most important part of your preparation,
even more so than packing and equipping, because your advance planning will insure the enjoyment and safety of each
member of your family on the wilderness expedition.

Planning

There are always many considerations to keep in mind when
you are deciding just where you will go on your wilderness trip.
Your kids will require a few more considerations. My first suggestion is to spend a great deal of time deciding where you will
go. This research takes time, but is time well spent. Having sent
for masses of material on different areas of interest to us, my
husband and I have spent many a rainy Sunday afternoon or
winter evening reading through the material, sharing our ideas,
and mulling over all the possibilities available to us. Take your

time, and choose carefully. Your choice can make or break your trip's success from nearly every angle: enjoyment, comfort, cost and, most important, safety.

These are some of the prerequisites we bear in mind when considering a location. Depending upon your special needs and interests, I'm sure you will want to add some to suit your own family.

1. Remoteness

Any parent of a very young child is aware of the swiftness with which illness can strike. One morning the child can appear healthy, but by suppertime she can be running a fever of 102° or more. If you have older children, you know how injuries can sometimes occur even under the most controlled conditions. First aid and safety precautions are of the utmost importance, and will be discussed in another chapter. But the first safety consideration should be this: Can we get out in a hurry if we have to? A further point on the subject—if one adult should be injured, could the other evacuate both adults and children effectively and quickly?

In other words, with children as members of your party, I consider it advisable to penetrate the wilderness, but not too deeply. Save the truly remote trips for the time when your family is more mature, or attempt them only in large parties where members of the group have a good background of experience, or in an area where the presence of forest rangers helps to insure your safety.

Don't be discouraged, though, because there is an infinite number of camping trips available which are well away from the intrusion of civilization, but not so far away to be dangerous. Your choice of location is more difficult because you are bringing the family, but you will still have a great variety of possibilities to choose from.

2. Difficulty

Choosing a trip which is within your capabilities not only makes the trip safer for your group, but the confidence you gain in choosing a goal you know you can accomplish will probably make your trip more enjoyable as well.

In canoe camping, the question of difficulty generally refers to the type of water you will have to navigate. Is it flat or rapid? If rapid, how severe? If severe, could the rapids be easily carried around?

In backpacking or bicycling, how rough is the terrain? How steep the gradient? Is it feasible with children if you plan on making just a limited distance each day? Or, is it feasible at all?

If you will be ski touring, are you assured of warm accommodations for the night? If snow conditions change, if the trails ice up or are exposed by melting snow, can you find alternate trails which would make the route easier?

No matter what type of trip you're considering—hiking, skiing, canoeing or bicycling—be sure to evaluate your ability and experience honestly. Again, this will in no way detract from your trip, unless the goal is to impress your armchair-athlete friends when you return home. An easy trip is as much or more fun than one which is difficult.

Find out as much as you can about the difficulty of any trip you consider by consulting any of the sources I will discuss later in the chapter, or by using the experience of another **reliable** camper. I stress the word reliable, because the egos of some people make them tend to either exaggerate or belittle the obstacles encountered on any given trip. One day in study hall my husband overheard some students retelling the tales a fellow teacher had told of an arduous-sounding canoe trip in Maine. Another student responded, "Aw, it couldn't have been that rough. Dorsey did it with his baby, for crying out loud!'' We did, and it was one of the simplest and most relaxing trips we've taken. On the other hand, we have a couple of friends whose extreme competence tends to make every trip they describe sound easy. So, seek out a reliable source, and take the words of others with several grains of salt!

If you can't find enough information concerning the difficulty of the trip to satisfy you, it is probably a good idea to find a different trip. And, for your first trip particularly, don't rule out a semi-wilderness location, possibly one quite near home. It will make a good testing ground for your family, and you might like it well enough to return on another occasion when travel time is limited. One of our most enjoyable overnight trips was on a river where we put in the canoe less than two miles from our house!

3. Proximity

How long will it take to get your location, and how long to get back home again? This may or may not be a factor to you, depending upon the amount of time you have for your vaca-

tion, how much money you have available for transportation, how well your family tolerates travel. The time spent in the car definitely cuts into your time spent in the wilderness; so you may want to find a trip requiring a certain reasonable length of time travelling. Chances are very good that you will be able to find an enjoyable and reasonably remote location without having to travel more than a few hours by car and/or public transportation.

4. Points of Interest

How suited is this area to your interests, and those of the adults and the children in your family? Is there the likelihood of good fishing? Are there good swimming areas, especially for children? Are there trails for hiking around camp? What are the chances for observing unusual birds and wildlife? Perhaps there are areas of geological or historic interest. For example, if your wife or older son is a history buff, a trip on the North Branch of the Dead River in Maine, along part of Arnold's route to Quebec, might have a significant appeal.

To find out about the possibilities for wilderness trip locations in your area, or in the part of the country you want to explore, there are several types of sources to investigate. Magazines dealing with outdoor sports and travel often contain articles describing various trips. Books on your favorite sport may also offer suggestions worth exploring. To get more information about any area that interests you, you can continue your search by investigating other sources.

The best place to start is probably to write to the information bureau of the state (or province) that interests you. Each state has a different title for the department or departments dealing with information of this sort. For example, let's assume you are interested in finding a canoe trip in Maine. In the state of Maine, the Forestry Department, State Parks and Recreation Commission, and the Department of Inland Fisheries and Game all dispense pertinent information, including excellent vacation planners. By writing a letter stating your plans and purposes, you can request any information available, including the names of any local organizations of canoeists, hikers, bicyclists, or ski-tourers, since these groups can provide you with still more helpful information. It is also a good idea to ask how to go about finding information on conditions just prior to your trip, since extreme water levels, lack of snow or road construction may cause you to want to change your plans at the last minute.

Address your letter to State Office Building, State Capitol, State, Zip, and note on the **outside** of the envelope the nature of the information you seek. Inside, be sure to mention when you plan to take the trip, so they can take into consideration the variables of certain trails and rivers according to the time of year.

Next, you can consult your library or bookstore for guidebooks describing the area. These are often published by such organizations as the Appalachian Mountain Club or the Sierra Club, but many are also individually produced. They generally give a very detailed description of roads, trails and waterways, giving you a good idea of the difficulty of your proposed trip.

Stores specializing in wilderness sports, or outfitters in the area you want to explore, may also have valuable information about trips you may want to take. Many times they are willing to give you some information and advice even if you are not bringing your business to them. Advocates of wilderness sports are often so enthusiastic about their favorite trips, they enjoy talking about them at any given opportunity. Of course, if you plan to use a guide, he will provide you with any information you seek on the area through which he will be taking you. Lists of guides can also be obtained from state agencies. We have never used a guide ourselves, and I don't feel they are necessary as long as your party includes at least one person who is knowledgeable in the use of map and compass, and as long as proper care and precautions are taken. But, if you are setting off to explore an area in a region which is foreign to you in climate, terrain, and wildlife, you may be safer and more comfortable travelling with a guide who is familiar with the peculiarities of the region.

While state agencies, environmental organizations and individually produced guidebooks generally offer an abundance of information to the canoeist or backpacker in any given part of the country, you may have considerably more trouble finding out about the trips available to you when setting out by bicycle or on skis. In the New England area, bicycle tripping in remote areas seems to be the hardest to learn about. Many undeveloped areas are traversed by roads and, if you don't object to travelling some distance on dirt roads, you can often find a good campsite off the beaten path. Most of the trips discussed in the guidebooks I have seen deal with urban and suburban locations—hardly good locations for camping expeditions. The availability of information varies greatly in different parts of the country, but your best bet is probably the local bicycling organization. Again, the state agencies can be most helpful in helping you locate this group, or you may seek the information from your own local bicycling organization, or from a periodical on the subject.

If ski touring is your type of trip, probably the best overview of areas, including a review of camping or hostel accommodations, is the annual yearbook on cross-country skiing published by *Ski* magazine. This gives a brief description of a vast number of areas for ski touring in all parts of the country, as well as many Canadian areas. After you have found several areas with distance, accommodations and level of difficulty to suit you, you can write to the sources listed for further information. You might be able to find local guidebooks at your bookstore or outfitter. Trail guides for backpackers can also provide ideas, if ski information is scarce for your area.

Lastly, maps are important in your planning stage, and an absolute necessity for your trip. Topographic maps showing elevation are the only kind that can allow you to judge the difficulty of the trip as a whole and the difficulty of any given section, because they show the gradient you will have to ascend and descend. These can often be obtained from book stores, outfitters, or mail order catalogs. If you're stuck, you can order them directly from the U.S. Geological Survey, 1200 South Eads Street, Arlington, Virginia 20202.

In the following chapters we will zero in on specialized equipment for all the self-propelled outdoor pursuits. This is a good place, however, to point out some basic equipment necessary for all wilderness family camping experiences.

Shelter

Some sort of shelter is necessary, even if you are planning to stay in areas where there are such facilities as hostels, huts, or shelters. Many will choose to bring a *lightweight tent*. Even if there are Adirondack type shelters available, in the height of bug season you will be more comfortable in a tent with mesh-covered openings. If you are winter camping, the small confines of a tent make a warmer place to spend the night than the spaciousness of an unheated hut. The typical backpacker's tent is a small, lightweight structure of two parts. The main body of the tent is made of rip-stop nylon, an extremely light material which resists mildew and rotting. The door to the tent is usually furnished with a covering of mosquito netting with a zippered closure, and a panel of rip-stop which can be zipped over to cover the netting. This panel is designed to keep out weather, and is also used to keep out those tiny insects known as "no-see-ums," who are small enough to fit through the openings in the mesh and deliver a needle-sharp sting.

Some manufacturers produce a "mosquito tent" which has the main body of the tent composed of mosquito netting. The idea of spending a July night in no-see-um country in such a tent could inspire many an H. G. Wells-type nightmare. The tent is usually supported by a frame of lightweight tubular aluminum, although some are supported simply by taut nylon lines and stakes. Tent frames may be either interior or exterior. An interior frame can decrease the efficiency of the space inside the tent, but most of

Tarp being set as a lean-to shelter with ground cloth beneath.

Lightweight tent for family backpacking.

the tents made by reputable manufacturers are well planned and officiont, whether they employ the interior or exterior frame. Since rip-stop nylon is not water repellent, the main body of the typical mountain tent requires additional protection. This is provided by a fly of coated nylon which is erected over the main body of the tent. Tent and fly usually share the same frame and, since the materials in both are extremely lightweight, the combination weighs considerably less than the tent used for car camping.

You may ask why the main body of the tent is not made of coated nylon itself, eliminating the need for a separate fly. Some economy tents are made in this manner, but the classic mountain tent consists of the two parts because this combination has proven to be the best suited for meeting the problems of confinement in a small enclosed area. The rip-stop breathes: it allows condensed water vapor and perspiration to escape through the material, while the coated fly protects the campers from rain. In a coated tent, the material does not breathe, so moisture is collected inside the tent, to the discomfort of the campers.

A relatively new material, *Gore-Tex®*, is used by some tent manufacturers to eliminate the need for both tent and fly. *Gore-Tex®* is made by stretching the resin from which *Teflon®* is made into a thin membrane. This material itself is too thin and flexible to hold up to rugged use, so it is laminated between two layers of fabric. The *Gore-Tex*®-laminated fabric is both water-proof and vapor porous. Sounds impossible? It seems that water vapor molecules are much smaller than those of liquid water. So, while the holes in the membrane will allow water vapor to escape out, they are too tiny to allow rain in. This fabric is expensive, but is probably the biggest recent development in camping equipment and clothing. While early laminates were criticized for being vulnerable to damage from wear and soils, the new improved version, *Gore-Tex II*® is highly reputed.

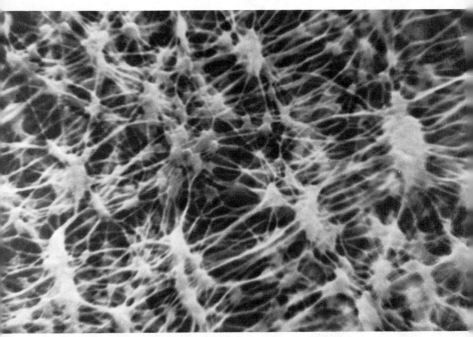

A close-up of Gore-Tex® membrane. This lightweight fabric breathes, yet does not absorb moisture.

The size of the tent you require can be a concern if you are used to car camping. One seldom sees tents of any kind in campgrounds accessible to the highway nowadays. When a tent is seen, it is usually of gigantic proportions. Our next door neighbors recently purchased a new tent which is about as big as their living room, and complete with a front porch. If you are used to tents like this, you may well be shocked when you tour the wilderness camping stores and see the tiny compact tents they have set up which are marked "two-man," "three-man," even "four-man." But to those of us used to wilderness camping, it is the living room-sized tent that looks ludicrous. After all, we are not going camping to spend our time sitting in the tent. The tent is used purely for sleeping. Even on a rainy day, just put on your rain clothes, go outside and make the best of things. It's bound to be more fun than sitting in a lawn chair in a large tent playing a card game. All you need is room to comfortably fit everyone's sleeping bags.

A *lightweight fly* can substitute for a tent adequately if the season is not buggy, or it can supplement a tent as a piece of optional equipment that is nice to include if weight and bulk are not critical. It is simply a square or rectangular piece of coated nylon fabric with loops or grommets for rigging it with ropes. It is quite light and compact. If you have more room than money, you may substitute a sheet of heavy-duty polyethylene and some grommets from your local outfitter. These grommets can be adhesive-backed, or they may be a garter-type arrangement with metal loops and rubber balls, ingeniously fitted together to provide a reusable grommet for attaching the fly to a rope or cord.

The fly will provide a dry place for preparing and eating food in rainy weather, and a spot where an infant can stay dry and yet still be able to see what's going on. Some optimistic parents even seem to think their children will play under the fly on a rainy day. I have learned not to expect this to be one of its purposes. It's hard to deny a child the fun of exploring as long as there are warm, dry clothes available so that she can warm up if necessary.

Cooking

A *nesting cook kit* can be purchased or put together on your own according to your individual needs. This should include a *fry pan, two pots* (of different sizes so they may be nested), a *plate, cup* and *set of utensils* for each member of the family, a *spatula* and a *sharp knife*. Other items you need that relate to food preparation may also be crammed inside the cook set, as many as will fit. Those that do not fit in the cook set may be stuffed into the pockets of packs. These necessary items include *matches* (in a waterproof container), *water purification tablets* (iodine or halazone), *dish soap, scrubber, dish towel, pot holder* and *pot gripper*. By pot holder, I refer to a padded cloth or mit used to grasp hot pots and pans, while a pot gripper is a handle which can be applied either by squeezing pincer parts together on the edge of a pan, or by hooking onto a specially provided attachment on the side of a pot.

Rather than bringing a knife and can opener, a well-chosen Swiss Army-type knife can be included. Depending on your needs, the gadgets of the knife can include several sizes of blade, can opener, nail file, cork screw, fish scaler, awl, scissors, small saw, screwdrivers *ad infinitem*—even a plastic toothpick! These knives are not just gimmicks: The model we own also has flat and Phillips-head screwdrivers for bikes or ski binding repairs.

A *water container* is needed for carrying water from the spring or water source, for holding the water while the purification tablets are at work, or for carrying water along with you if you are not assured of water sources along the way. If you are backpacking and bringing water along, you will probably want a water bag designed to fit easily into a pack. If you are canoeing, or travelling in an area where you are assured of the presence of fresh water, a collapsible plastic water jug holding about $2\frac{1}{2}$ gallons is probably the best bet.

The compact *one-burner stove* is scoffed at by many who fancy themselves latter-day voyageurs and who consider cooking over an open fire the only true way to camp. But the camp stove is becoming more and more important as the interests of ecology become indelibly inscribed in our minds. Increased numbers of wilderness campers mean increased land use in certain areas. The wood lots around many popular wilderness campsites simply cannot supply unlimited resources to campers dependent upon wood fires. Many areas, particularly those in the West, categorically restrict the use of wood fires for any but emergency purposes. And, in any part of the country, a dry season like that of the early summer of 1976 means a ban on wood fires, period. Even if regulations allow them, you may find yourself at a campsite where either there is no fuel available nearby, or there is no safe spot to build a fire without seriously defacing the appearance of the area. A camp stove is no longer a luxury, it's a practicality.

The three most common fuels on the market are propane, butane, and white gas. Butane and propane have a definite advantage if you will be tripping with young children, because they are safer to have with you. A fuel bottle of gasoline is so lothal such a small amount can kill a youngster—I cannot feel comfortable with one in my pack. Propane is a more efficient fuel than butane in extremely cold weather, so if you will be doing much winter camping you may want to keep this in mind. It also can be bought in bulk tanks and used to fill refillable cartridges to fit the stove. Make sure any cartridge you attempt to refill is made for this purpose, however, since some can be refilled while most others must be disposed of after the one use. If you do choose to bring gasoline, make sure your fuel bottle is not apt to be mistaken for anything besides fuel, and that it is kept away from any young children or pets. Another stove on the market, for the camper who must travel light (the backpacker, bicyclist or skier) or the canoeist on a very long extended trip, is one which may be used with a variety of different fuels—gas, Sterno, charcoal—even wood chips. Since there are almost always some wood scraps available near any forest campsite, this stove is worthy of investigation.

Bedding

The number of sleeping bags and mattresses needed for your party will vary according to both the number of people in your party, and the size of those people. The first year we brought a little camper along (our five-month-old daughter), my husband, baby and I all slept together in two adult bags zippered together, atop two knee-length foam pads. Later, our one- and two-year-old daughters slept in the same adult bag, with heads sticking out at opposite ends! By ages three and four, they each had their own bags, but shared a foam pad laid horizontally beneath their bags. If you are bringing sub-adult size campers, you may want to experiment to find the least heavy, least bulky combination of sleeping equipment with which your family will be comfortable.

If you will be purchasing bags and/or mattresses for the first time, or if you are replacing old equipment, keep in mind that your interests, and particularly those of your children as they get older, are subject to change. If you buy equipment which is only suited for your needs as you see them now, you may end up having to re-equip sooner than would otherwise be necessary. So, even if you think you will never camp in winter, it may be worth a few more dollars to buy a sleeping bag which is adequate for reasonably low temperatures.

The three insulating materials which are used most frequently for filling quality sleeping bags are down, *Dacron II*®, and *Polar Guard*®. The first is a natural product, the down of either geese or ducks. Goose down is the superior of the two, but both are extremely efficient in warmth and resiliency (50% more efficient than the closest substitute). By this, I mean that a bag of another material would have to weigh about 50% more to still provide the same warmth and loft. These statistics are impressive, and explain why down has been a classic, a favorite of the backpacker for many years.

But, in the past few years, the makers of the synthetic fillers have been doing a lot of work, and they have come up with some advantages of their own. First, of course, is price. A good synthetic bag can be purchased fairly inexpensively. Another, of particular interest to the canoeist, or to the camper whose bag keeps getting wet in the **60–40** tent we discussed a while back, is that the synthetic bag dries out in a small fraction of the time it takes for the down bag to do so. The most important advantage—and this is peculiar to only one synthetic, *Polar Guard*®—is that it retains its insulating qualities even when wet. Since my family spends a great deal of time camping by canoe, we chose *Polar Guard*® bags when we had to buy some new equipment last year, even though we did have to sacrifice a bit in the weight department.

Many people regard the use of a mattress as a bit of a luxury, if not downright soft. This is not true. A foam mattress has another function to perform for the camper besides that of comfort. A foam mattress protects the sleeping camper from ground cold by providing an additional layer of insulating material. It performs this function more efficiently than the air mattress, as well as being a heck of a lot more convenient and, in my opinion, more comfortable. Most people buy what are called $\frac{3}{4}$-length pads, mattresses which are being 42 and 52 inches wide. This provides a cushion for the top part of your body; you really don't need any under your legs, although longer mattresses are available if you really want one that is full length. The mattresses are quite compressible and can be rolled tightly and tied onto a pack, or stuffed, as we do, into a sack along with the sleeping bag.

Clothing

Clothing can be a problem to a beginning camper. As a tourist or car camper, you may be used to bringing a lot of clothes. Even if asked to reduce that number, you may still have in mind several changes of clothes. But, if you are going to fit your family's clothing in a pack or duffel along with other pieces of equipment, you are going to have to completely revise your thinking. With a couple of clean sets of underwear and pairs of socks thrown in, the clothing you would bring on a day trip should also be sufficient for an extended trip. You can bring along a small supply of laundry detergent (biodegradable, please) and wash out underwear or tee shirts and socks, so you won't need a fresh pair from home for each day. Jeans will look dirty five minutes from the time you put them on, so it makes little difference whether you bring one pair or more, except that it is heavier if each person brings more. You may, however, want to bring a pair of cut-offs as well as full-length jeans. As well as giving you an optional outfit in case of very warm weather, this will allow you to include your dirty jeans in with your laundry, if they have become unbearably cruddy.

Babies and very young children will need more clothing than the older kids and adults, but luckily their clothes are so tiny that the additional number shouldn't crowd the pack too much. For babies, stretch suits that cover from neck to toe are great to bring camping. They are compact, comfortable, easy to wash out, and provide good coverage for protection from the sun and insects. If you can find some that will dry out quickly in a good breeze, five of these suits will probably be sufficient. Wool sweaters and a blanket sleeper can be layered over the suits to provide warmth. A warm cap or bonnet for the occasional cool, windy day even in mid-summer, a hat with a brim to protect the face from exposure to the sun, and a little windbreaker with a hood round out baby's camping wardrobe. You may also want to include some waterproof pants, even if you are bringing disposable diapers with a plastic layer, since these are known to leak on occasion.

Ah, yes—diapers. The summer that marked our first year without diapers was indeed refreshing. Since our children were born only fifteen months apart, we may have set the world's record for the number of disposable diapers portaged on a canoe trip that first summer we travelled with the two of them. We started out with a huge duffel bag filled with nothing but diapers! I strongly recommend disposable diapers. In fact, I can't imagine a camping trip with diapers that need to be laundered. Who wants to spend a vacation dreaming fondly of the laundromat? Disposable diapers are truly a lifesaver, although they are a bit more difficult to dispose of in the wilds. There are some brands, other than those nationally advertised, which have no plastic layer. You can provide your own waterproof pants and wash them out. They dry quickly, so this shouldn't present a problem. The diaper itself can then be either burned or buried. If you must use the type of disposable diaper with the attached plastic layer, you

can separate this layer after the diaper is used and carry the plastic out with the rest of your trash. The paper part can then be burned or buried like the former kind of diaper. If you choose burning, it is preferable to burn the diapers the last thing at night, or just before you break camp in the morning and extinguish your fire, since they produce an unpleasant odor not conducive to fireside chats and visits. For this reason, and because a soggy diaper takes such a long time to dry out and burn, many people prefer to bury them. They should be treated in the same manner one would treat any human waste—buried away from streams, lakes and other water sources, buried deeply enough so they will not be easily dug up by animals.

The toddler needs a few more clothes than his older sister or borther, too. I generally bring two shirts (one with long sleeves, one with short), two wool sweaters and one windbreaker for each child. The number of dungarees depends upon how well the toilet training has been going! If the child has progressed to the only-an-occasional-accident stage, three pair will probably be sufficient, since you can rinse them out and dry them. Pants, both over and under, that dry quickly are a boon, and those thick training pants that most of us use regularly at home are probably best left there in the drawer. One rainy week when we were having bathroom problems with our older daughter, we spent a good part of the week toasting training pants on a stick over the fire in an attempt to dry them out! When we returned home, the first thing I did was head for the store for some fast-drying underwear. Fairly heavy socks are preferable to the little nylon and cotton pair they wear at home in the summertime, since they are sturdier, warmer, and less penetrable by insects. And don't forget the hats—a wide brim and wool cap. In the northern states, a warm cap is often needed on a breezy night, even in July or August.

When packing clothes, it is helpful to put each individual's clothing in a sack of a different color. This makes things a lot simpler anytime there's more than just one or two of you on a trip. If you don't want to invest in stuff sacks, you may use pillowcases of different colors and patterns for clothes bags.

Rain gear can help to guarantee your vacation. With adequate protection, even bad weather can't spoil your fun! A poncho, a two-piece rain suit (jacket and pants), or a long hooded shirt called a cagoule offers protection from the elements. For children, it is often hard to find a lightweight rain outfit in a small size. If you're ambitious, you may want to make one for your youngster out of coated nylon, using a commercially available jacket pattern with a hood. Either make it knee length, or make a pair of simple pants with an elasticized waist out of the same material, and your little one will be all set for playing in the rain.

There are several new clothing products and materials that can substantially reduce the number of articles of clothing you put in your pack. First is the development of polypropylene undergarments. This material wicks moisture away from the body and dries extremely fast. A turtleneck shirt of this material is not only more efficient than cotton long underwear, it's also attractive enough to double as undershirt or shirt—especially if you choose a bright color.

Similarly *fiberpile garments*- vests, jackets or sweaters—retain much warmth when wet, and dry quickly. A good wringing alone will get rid of most wetness, even after a dunking. This material is also often used for booties, mits and balaclava hats.

Gore-Tex II®, a laminated fabric discussed under tents, is used to make excellent mountain parkas that can double as rain jackets and wind-breakers. Similarly, pants made of this material are good to wear either in rainy or extremely windy conditions.

Unfortunately, few of these new clothing products are yet available for children. Hopefully that situation will soon change so the whole family can enjoy the benefits of these new developments.

If you are ambitious, creative, innovative and/or resourceful you may be interested in manufacturing your own camp clothing and equipment such as tents, flies and sleeping bags. A number of companies sell kits for these items as well as day packs, bicycle panniers and other paraphernalia. In addition, many mail order houses sell the basic materials and notions such as zippers, nylon thread, straps and grommets. Books and patterns can be located to assist in making your own gear. As well as saving money, some folks find this rewarding in its own right.

Generally I prefer to shop the end-of-season sales and the "bargain basements" some of the larger outfitters feature. Here you can often find mark-downs and seconds, or simply discontinued items, which could be superior to what you produce on your own.

The Campsite

What should you look for when you choose a spot for an overnight stopover, or a vacation "home away from home"? First of all, seek out a large enough level spot to set your tent. You should avoid low hollows where water would settle in wet weather. Be sure to avoid open, exposed places which might become dangerous in thunderstorms. If your tent needs to be staked, look for ground that will accept stakes, rather than soft sand or ledge.

Consider the trip as a peaceful holiday with your children. Keep in mind that everything you do in the environment should teach them to respect your campsite as your outdoor home and disturb your surroundings as little as possible. This concept of "minimum impact use" should be foremost in the mind of all campers. Some of the old camping traditions are no longer accepted practices and are illegal in many areas.

For example, campers should obviously not cut standing trees or drive nails into them. Trenching, the digging of shallow trenches around the tent to avoid the problem of standing water, is not acceptable either. Campfires are now outlawed in many areas and are taboo in any wilderness location during a dry season. Portable gasoline, propane or butane stoves have largely replaced the campfire for cooking and, where campfires are illegal or dangerous, a candle lantern will have to provide the romance. Rather than feeling hampered by such restrictions, the conscientious camper should feel good about experiencing nature while keeping it intact.

Once the tent is up, you may want to raise the fly (if you brought one along), either as a rain shelter for gathering and eating space, or an area to store your gear.

A clothesline set up at one end of your site can perform a variety of services: drying clothes, pinning small items that might be misplaced or left on the ground, keeping gear accessible to adults but out of reach of young children. A sock pinned to a high clothesline can form a childproof pocket for keeping matches or insect repellent.

Parachute cord is a good choice of line. This lightweight cord made of nylon will not rot and will last a camping family through many adventures. Inexpensive, it is available in many bright colors. Bright colors are convenient as well as attractive: you're less apt to either walk into the line or leave it behind!

Food and Waste

Good housekeeping is necessary even when wilderness camping. All litter must be disposed of properly. That means packing back out with you all that you cannot safely burn. Food must always be enclosed in sealed bags and containers to avoid attracting raccoons or other scavenging animals.

Dishes should always be thoroughly washed and put away after each meal. To neglect this chore is to invite stomach disturbances, insects and hungry animals. A clean campsite is usually pest-free, but a messy site is an invitation to unwanted wildlife visitors. Also, think of how much you would want to arrive at a messy campsite after a long paddle.

Children should be taught at an early age that human waste must be adequately buried. A folding shovel or a simple garden trowel should be included in your pack for this purpose.

Sundries

A small *mending kit* can prevent the small accident from becoming a major inconvenience, and takes almost no room at all in the pack. A spool of heavy-duty thread and a needle tucked into a plastic film container are sufficient.

If you will be building a wood fire at all, you will probably want to include a folding *saw,* and possibly an *ax,* too. A saw is a tool which is valuable in a survival-type situation, so many people consider it an absolute necessity. I must confess that in familiar territory, we often trip without one. There is a pocket saw on the market which consists of a chain with a ring on either end, taking up very little space and costing very little money. How efficiently this saw functions is debatable, but if you want to bring along a saw chiefly for survival purposes, this little model might be a good choice. If you decide to bring an ax, be sure it is properly sheathed.

You will want to include a *flashlight* in your pack, and possibly additional flashlights for the children in your party who are old enough to use them. We bought them for our children largely for reasons of self-defense. They were driving us crazy wanting to use ours! But it is handy having more than one per family. Often one parent may be fishing until dark with one of the children while the others stay at camp toasting marshmallows over the campfire. Or, one parent may be setting up the sleeping bags in the tent while the other takes the children for the last visit to the outhouse or woods. A small folding candle lantern can be a cozy addition to your camp also, especially if you are in an area where fires are prohibited.

Personal gear you will need in your travels includes toothbrushes, toothpaste, soap, laundry detergent, towels and toilet paper. If you're bringing diapers, the disposable, pre-moistened towelettes are also handy to bring along, and can help avoid diaper rash. If your baby's sensitive, though, you'd better bring along your favorite rash remedy, too.

Protection from the sun and from insects is also very important. A *sun screen,* a cream or lotion which completely blocks out the sun's harmful rays, may be needed by even those who consider themselves thick-skinned. And it is just plain thick-headed to travel in late spring, summer or early fall without *repellent*! Brands containing a large percentage of N-Diethylmetatoluamide are the most effective, but can harm some fabrics; so they should be used carefully. And, as I mentioned earlier, I think the lotion forms are far superior to the aerosols, and better for the environment, too. A friend of ours who likes to frequent the backwoods of New Hampshire once gave us a recipe for his own special fly dope:

1 ounce citronella
2 ounces cedar leaf oil
12 ounce spirit of camphor.

We made a batch and used it on a canoe trip in May. It was great—it didn't even wash off on our hands when they got wet paddling. The only trouble was that about a week after our return home, I was still trying to wash it off!

Other items you will need to bring along on your trip which are discussed at length in other parts of this book are a *first-aid kit* and *manual, maps* and a *compass,* and *food.* A combination of miscellaneous equipment to accommodate your own special needs and interests will round out your pack. These may include a camera, binoculars, books (pleasure reading, wildlife guides, etc.) and a sketchbook. Some new items to our pack trips are my husband's harmonica, my recorder, and a couple of kazoos for the kids. I don't know how much our wilderness neighbors appreciate our campfire concerts, but we certainly enjoy them!

These items, and waterproof duffels and/or packs to contain them, comprise the basic equipment you will need for your family's wilderness adventure. If you're trying this type of camping for the first time and are hesitant to invest, there are outfitters and rental agencies throughout the country that can help equip you for your first trip. And I'll bet you'll enjoy that trip enough to start saving your pennies or heading for the wilderness equipment store the minute you return home!

"How do You Manage?"

This is the biggest question I'm always asked whenever I'm talking about tripping in the wilderness with my little girls, whether the questioner is a mother who indignantly insists she would **never** take her baby camping, or the wistful parent I meet on a camping trip who misses the little toddler he or she left behind in the charge of a baby-sitter. First of all, to *"manage"* you have to adopt a certain essential philosophy if you are all to have fun. It is basically this: You are not at home, so don't try to live as though you were. Clean faces and clothes that look like they should appear on a Clorox commercial are not the order of the day. If you try to keep your children looking that way when they are playing in the dirt all day, you will be miserable and so will they. Don't follow them around all day with a wash cloth. Let them have a good time. Besides, during insect season, you won't want to repeatedly wash off their repellent. If you clean them carefully a couple of times a day, maybe after breakfast and just before bed, you will at least feel the assurance that the dirt you are seeing is newly acquired! Of course, there are extenuating circumstances, and if your child **wants** to be cleaned up, you might as well oblige if it can be done. In most cases, though, if you don't act fussy about it, neither will the child. Remember—you'll all have time to go home and have a long, hot bath before Grandma sees you!

As at home, the basic rule with toddlers is simply to watch them at all times. This is a lot easier to do when camping than it is at home, since you're always together, usually sharing the same activities. Be sure no one leaves any sharp utensils such as an ax or a knife within reach. First-aid kits, insect repellents, and fishing tackle likewise have to be kept away from small hands. And don't forget that some things have to be protected **from** the toddler. You have limited supplies of food and fuel, so make sure they're well away from the children. This business is a bit more complicated away from closets, shelves and cupboards, but things may be hung from trees, and stuffing forbidden objects deep into a pack where it will take awhile to get at them will provide a sort of early-warning system.

I've often been asked what kinds of toys we bring along when we camp. My answer—as few and simple as possible. From observing my own children and others, I've found that lots of toys are not only unnecessary, but downright detrimental. If you bring toys, the children will spend most of their time playing with their toys, and that's not what I take mine along to do. Toys represent a whole segment of life which helps to divorce us from the wilderness. I read an article in a woman's magazine about "family camping" with young children. This article, however, discussed paved campground camping where the otherwise bored kiddies would be entertained by clowns, organized games, sing-a-longs, hay rides, plus the myriad of toys, books and board games which parents were adviced to bring from home, along with the port-a-crib and playpen. Ugh! This may be a fine vacation for some people, but it's not what I have in mind, and I doubt that it's what you have in your mind, either.

The summer we camped with a five-month-old infant we brought only one toy—a "jolly jumper"—which we moved from tree to tree as we changed campsites. It filled the bill perfectly—it was fairly light and compact, it gave our daughter exercise, and it added to her enjoyment of the environment rather than de- tracted from it. With toddlers, we generally bring only a small pail and shovel for each. I'm not even sure these are necessary, but the pails are handy for carrying the endless collection of pine- cones, sticks and stones. When our older daughter was four, she brought along a little backpack with a shovel and her flashlight in it. (The rest of the pack contained her clothing, to which she added some of the treasures she finds.) Children find their own games outdoors, when they are not hampered by too many little plastic trucks and dolls from home. They will build with the rocks and branches they find, write and draw on the ground with sticks and invent all sorts of games of their own.

Infants do require a few special considerations, but are really nice camping companions. The first is their food. The year we brought our tiny baby (she was six weeks old when we started the trip), we had it made. I was breast-feeding her, and she was not taking solids yet, so we had virtually no extra food to bring! If you have an infant on formula, things will be a bit more complicated, but it can still be done. Most of the manufacturers of prepared formulas produce a powdered form, although it may be hard to locate since most people use the liquid concentrates. If you plan ahead, your druggist can probably order it for you. Prepare each bottle of formula as it is needed, never trying to store it from one feeding to the next. Without refrigeration bacteria build up very quickly in a medium such as a baby's formula. Even nursing mothers, by the way, are wise to bring a small amount of powdered formula in case of an emergency. When using bottles, make sure they are scrupulously clean and boiled—this is not the place to be careless about health precautions. It is also not a good idea to keep baby food in a jar from one meal to the next. In fact, why bring baby food, except for the instant cereal. One of the pieces of baby equipment we used to bring everywhere, and which I cannot recommend highly enough, is a baby food grinder. This is a small utensil which grinds adult food into a paste palatable for infants. These gadgets are inexpensive (about $10) and you'll find them useful in the home and for eating in restaurants. I know many mothers who make baby food in a blender, and I've tried it, but I found this simple device much more satisfactory. We can take it with us literally everywhere. These grinders can be purchased in many department stores and in health food stores. You can find them in the mail order sections of women's magazines.

Another piece of equipment we used to bring, which I found I could live quite happily without when we forgot it one time, was the infant seat. You know—the molded plastic inclined seat that we all think is such a marvelous invention? The time it got left behind, I discovered that, by leaning against a tree or rock and sitting with my knees bent up before me, I could provide a comfortable arrangement for feeding my daughter her cereal. I sat with her straddling my stomach, her head supported by my

knees. She quite enjoyed it, and this turned out to be such a sociable arrangement, she was often fed this way even after our return home.

One worry many mothers of infants seem to have before they make the decision to try wilderness camping with their little ones, is that their babies may have problems sleeping. Most of the babies I've had the pleasure of camping with, both my own daughters and the children of our camping friends, behave little differently than they would at home. In fact, most of them don't really seem to care that they are someplace to which they are unaccustomed. If your baby has trouble sleeping through the night at home, chances are he will when you're camping, too. But it is unlikely that the trip itself will cause much upheaval or anxiety for your baby. After all, infants experience so many things which are new to them all the time, they are most likely better able than the rest of us to adjust to a change from the routine.

As They Get Older—

As children progress to the older toddler and early school ages, some new considerations arise. In some ways your camping will be easier—no diapers, bottles, kiddy-packs. But, as the kids get a little older and more independent, they also become harder to keep track of.

I strongly feel that children of all ages should be taught to stay near the camp. Even adults can become lost much more easily than most of us would think, and a cocky ten-year-old seems prone toward this type of accident. If children are taught from the beginning the importance of staying where they belong and the reasons behind it, a lot of potential problems can be avoided.

When my children were still toddlers, I tried to impress upon them the importance of staying with the adults, always staying where they could see either the tent or one of the adults in the group. Dressing the children in bright clothing helps. When they are very small, you may want to sew jingle bells to the clothing or affixing them to their shoelaces. No young child should ever be allowed out of sight of the adults for any reason, for it is easy to get lost in unfamiliar surroundings. Furthermore, kids are very inquisitive. They should be taught what to do in case they do become separated from the adult campers, but educated so that this information need never be used. Be very watchful of infants near fire.

The whistle is an important piece of equipment, but just how to introduce it to the child is a rather ticklish problem. The child who is old enough to use it (age three plus) has enough natural curiosity and just plain nosiness to want to try it out. So, it's very likely that, given this new safety equipment and instructions, he will intentionally try to get himself lost to try it out. The danger of this situation is that, once separated from his parents, he may panic and forget the procedure or, in his enthusiasm, may get himself lost to such an extent that the whistle doesn't help. The best solution my husband and I could agree upon was to give the whistle to the child at a very early age—say, one year old or eighteen months—with no instruction at all. Simply hang it on a thong around his neck or, if that makes you nervous, sew it to a sleeve with heavy thread. Let him play with it. Then, when he has reached the ripe old age of three, and the novelty of the whistle has worn off, tell him how it might be used to help in a situation where he might become separated from the adults. In such an emergency, the child should sit down immediately, as soon as he realizes that he is lost, and blow the whistle. A whistle is louder and requires less exertion than yelling. Rescue workers stress the importance of the lost individual remaining in one spot to wait for help. Having instructed your three-year-old, watch him diligently to make sure he never needs to use these instructions. With proper supervision, it is doubtful that the child will ever become lost. The few well-publicized cases of such events are statistically very small when you consider the number of children who spend time in the wilderness or who live in rural areas. But accidents do happen, and they should know what to do should they ever become separated from the group.

I personally feel that the possibility of injury or accident is far greater for the older child or the adolescent than for the younger child. Older kids are more daring, more independent, more eager to impress. This type of problem is more likely to present itself in a group, rather than a family situation, but more than one family travelling together with older children of the same age may have similar experiences. An explorer leader advises to watch out for the child who falls short of matching his peers in physical strength, stamina, swimming ability, or agility. He may feel compelled to try to keep up with them, and get himself into trouble. Once, in the Adirondacks, we shared a lake campsite with a co-ed group of scouts. I saw a fun game of tag nearly become a tragedy because one boy's swimming ability was not good enough to take part in the game, and he tried to fake it. Fortunately, their leader was alert to the situation, and all ended well.

As your children are given increased camp responsibilities, such as being allowed to carry a jackknife or help split the firewood, I think it is especially important to watch for signs of carelessness or abuse, and insist upon their learning and using safe procedures. A deep cut can be serious enough at home, but hours or days from the nearest hospital, it can be a real emergency. Make sure to teach them the proper methods of using camp tools, and insist that they use them correctly.

The typical family camping trip, even if it includes several families, tends to be a rather low-key affair, however, and problems with older children getting into trouble in the ways I've discussed will probably never materialize if the trip is kept on a congenial and non-competitive level. You'll probably all have a lot more fun that way. To me, that's the key right there: the object of all of this should be to have fun. If you relax and "**simplify, simplify,**" I think your children will get a much clearer picture of what the wilderness has to offer them and to all of us in terms of enjoyment and peace of mind.

3. GROWING OLDER

As your children grow older, their physical stamina increases and their abilities improve, especially if you've kept them active along the way. On the other hand, family activities begin to encounter a lot more competition from Little League, school activities, social events, and just hanging out with the neighborhood crowd.

Now you must face the problem of how to keep these older kids interested. One factor in your favor is that, while wilderness outings may be commonplace by now for your children, they are viewed as exciting and adventuresome by most of their friends. You can play up this angle by encouraging your child to share stories of your trips with pals and classmates.

A seashell souvenir from a four-day bike trip on Martha's Vineyard made my daughter the "star" of Show-and-Tell one day at school. On another occasion, I invited myself to show slides of a western backpacking trip to my other daughter's class when they were studying the Western states in Social Studies. She acted as narrator, and thoroughly enjoyed fielding the many questions of her fascinated schoolmates. Both experiences helped to increase the girls' appreciation of their own adventures out-of-doors, and gave them the feelings of acceptance and recognition so important in relationships with their peers.

When you finally get the slides from your trip back from the film processor—always an exciting occasion—you might schedule a party for several families which includes children of similar ages. Not only will this encourage your children's continued interest in your family excursions, but you might make some converts. That's always satisfying and can also provide some new companions for future trips. Or, you might choose to plan a children's party for the kids and their friends alone.

Probably the best way to liven up your child's trip is to supply more children. Bring along one of those envious classmates, a favorite cousin, or a neighborhood pal on a short, simple trip. Trip with another family or two. While this may appear to be a lot of added work and more responsibility for you, you'll probably find that the kids will entertain each other. That's more free time for yourselves.

Don't expect things to always run smoothly on such a trip. It's not that children are any more competitive than adults; it's just that they happen to be a lot less inhibited about showing it! Rivalries are bound to crop up. But, if you take such matters in stride, chances are that any difficulties will be short-lived.

A recent canoe trip included a friend and his son, who is just one year older than our older daughter, along with our family. The six of us played "musical chairs" between two canoes, switching positions about twice a day for two weeks. (Be careful about moving about or roughhousing in the canoe itself.) Various alliances were formed and reformed among the children. Jealousies and hurt feelings surfaced here and there, largely centering around the fact that the other kid caught all the fish! Although there were some difficult moments, all three kids emerged with a special friendship, the result of the period of time spent together in the wilds. When both families got together several weeks later to share pictures from the trip, the kids treated the occasion as a reunion of long-lost friends.

Another way you can sustain a child's interest in family outings is to encourage his active participation in every stage of the trip, beginning with planning. Allow your child to choose the activity or the location for some of your family adventures. Family members may even take turns planning activities, on a rotating

52

basis. We've tried this technique and found the grumbling much less audible when the Sunday afternoon canoe tour is on a river chosen by one child, while the other knows that her turn to choose will come next weekend.

For an extended trip, a child may enjoy helping to plan and pack equipment and meals, or being responsible for cooking breakfast before leaving home the first day.

During the trip, campsite chores such as tent-raising, cooking and cleanup, can be shared by all family members. If the trip involves hiking, bicycling or skiing, children will, of course, be actively involved throughout each day. Don't make the mistake of allowing them to become bored passengers on a canoe trip. You may even find it worthwhile to get hold of an additional canoe, if you must, to allow all children to be a part of paddling. Younger children can each paddle with an adult; two more experienced youngsters might even be happiest managing their own boat, bow and stern.

In general, if you treat the young campers as responsible members of the party, they will be more interested, less bored, and will feel a greater stake in the trip's success.

With your children more mature, you are now free to choose more adventurous routes. Maybe a little easy whitewater or more portages. A more demanding hike, or a winter camping trip on skis. Perhaps your bike route won't have to entirely exclude more heavily travelled roads.

Still, keep in mind that it's always preferable to err on the side of too easy. By keeping the demands of any family trip well within the abilities of each member, you can help insure getting an enthusiastic response next time you say "Let's go camping!"

4. OUTDOOR NOURISHMENT

The food that accompanies most wilderness campers would not thrill the likes of Julia Child or Craig Claiborne. It does not always thrill the likes of me, and it is always a treat when, the first night of our return home, we treat ourselves to a big steak, corn on the cob, cold beer, ice cream—those things we've been dreaming about. But the nonperishable camping food we take along is nutritious, relatively good tasting, and greatly appreciated when we are out on the trail. Some campers like to really go "gourmet" and cook some of the traditional voyageur foods like beans baked in a hole. I know some families and camp groups who think a reflector baker is indispensible, indeed, even a camp group that lugs along huge cans of cherry pie filling in order to bake pies for dessert in the reflector oven.

But I don't adhere to these ideas, and luckily my family goes along wth me. After all, the cook is on vacation also, and I get enough of a chance to cook and fuss over meals at home. When we're out in the woods, I'd much rather enjoy myself and spend the time fishing, swimming, relaxing, doing just about anything but spending a great part of the day cooking. So, we bring along simple meals, easy-to-fix meals, largely one-pot meals.

In planning foods to bring along, I think there are several important considerations, the first of which is nutrition. Although some outdoorsmen claim that on short trips (up to about a week's duration) nutrition is a luxury rather than an important criterion, I feel it's important since I generally feel much better and have a better time if the food I'm eating is nutritionally sound. And, with children along, I consider it important to keep them healthy and sound, and to keep up the good habits of nutrition which they are hopefully getting at home. Therefore, when I plan meals to bring on our trips, whether they are day trips, weekend outings, or extended camping trips, nutritional value is my first consideration.

Another important criterion is caloric intake, and this is especially important for the active outdoor family. Your food is the fuel which will enable your body to do the work you will be asking it to do—hiking, bicycling, skiing, paddling. It will be keeping you warm in cold and rainy weather, fit and alert in any clime. So bear this in mind when meal planning. Consult a caloric intake chart (*Good Housekeeping Cookbook for Calory Watchers* has a detailed chart outlining the daily recommendations of calories and of basic vitamins for all ages) and use it as a guide. But remember to take into consideration the amount of physical activity in which your family will be indulging. If you're planning a tough trip, you may need far more calories than those recommended for the average individual. And, if you're pregnant or nursing a baby, don't forget that these conditions greatly increase your caloric needs. It is undoubtedly best not to cut the caloric values of the foods you bring too closely. Sometimes I tend to be a little too stingy in this area. I guess I keep thinking of carrying those extra few ounces over the trail on my back. Unfortunately, when I do miscalculate, we all suffer for it.

Don't try to diet while on this type of trip. You'll probably lose a few pounds, anyway. If you are trying to cut down, you can avoid eating excessively, after you've had your fill, but be sure to eat enough to keep you going strong. Generally, a feeling of physical well-being will tell you you're on the right track. If you find yourself tiring easily or unable to perform well the tasks you know you can do, if you find yourself the first in the group to feel cold or fatigued, you should think back and ask yourself if you've been consuming enough calories. Since very young children cannot do this for themselves, and since older children may not keep these signs in mind, you will have to watch them for these telling signs.

Next, one must consider the perishability of the foods. Many foods have an infinite or near-infinite shelf life. Some will last up to a week with no problem, but should not be pushed to two. Many are just plain dangerous to bring because of their tendency toward spoilage. When you plan your meals, choose foods that will be sure to keep for a reasonable length of time, and make sure you have a schedule of meals which uses the foods with limited storage lives while they are still good.

The relative weight and bulk of the foods you bring will be of concern to any wilderness camper, especially the backpacker, bicyclist or skier. Even for the canoeist, the food pack must fit into the boat, and the portage trails will seem a lot shorter if you try to keep that pack as light and compact as possible.

As I mentioned before, another prime consideration of mine is time and ease of preparation. Even if you are not quite as lazy as I am, this is important, especially if your cooking will be largely confined to a camp stove. The longer the food has to cook, the more fuel you will need to pack along. That, to me, is the major inconvenience of the reflector oven. The cooking fire needed to simmer a pot of spaghetti or the like is minimal. A bunch of driftwood or "squaw wood" will suffice for that. But, to bake even a simple pan of biscuits in a reflector baker requires a big fire, usually involving splitting a large quantity of wood with an ax. Unless you will be travelling in areas where firewood is plentiful, unless you are willing to work hard for your cake or brownies, unless you are willing to carry an ax and saw along, think twice about taking in this type of setup. On trips where weight is not much of a factor, and where we might feel like baking, my family brings along a little eight-inch cast iron Dutch oven. It's no light weight, so it stays home a lot, but it requires only the remaining coals from the supper fire to cook a batch of biscuits or corn bread. Being the loafers that we are, it suits our camping style better!

The consideration of time and ease of preparation also eliminates such foods as dried peas and bean dishes, which can be highly nutritious and tasty, but require a long cooking time.

Putting all these considerations together will limit the number of different types of foods you bring. But then it's not always the restaurant with the long menu that has the greatest appeal, right? You have to pay some price for atmosphere, after all, and I think that the atmosphere in which you'll be consuming these meals will make them rate with your favorite delicacies. Just keep telling yourself that!

Most outfitters and camping stores can fix you up with convenient and tasty freeze-dried foods. The variety is astounding. From the various companies producing this kind of stuff, you may pick anything from shrimp cocktail and beef stroganoff to freeze-dried ice cream, no less! Some brands even are available in foil pouches in which the meals are prepared by simply adding a small amount of boiling water. They can even be eaten from the pouch, enabling you to leave several items from the mess kit at home.

But freeze-dried food is very expensive, and probably won't be practical for you if your budget is limited. If you can spend some extra weight and some extra time, you can package your own nonperishable meals from supermarket materials and, while I can't promise you shrimp cocktail and ice cream, the meals will be tasty and pleasing. A typical day's menu might be something like this:

Breakfast—	granola with dried fruit
	reconstituted non-fat dry milk
	cocoa (the just-add-water type)
Lunch—	peanut butter spread (mixture of peanut butter, powdered milk, honey and cococoanut flakes)
	party rye bread or whole-grain crackers
	Tang or Wyler's
	gorp (equal parts peanuts or roasted soy beans, raisins, M&M's)
Supper—	packaged macaroni and cheese dinner with ham-flavored vegetable protein bits
	instant vegetable soup
	Tang or Wyler's
	instant pudding made with instant dry milk

Since you will probably have to investigate several super-markets to find your provisions, allow plenty of time for collecting food items in advance of your trip. However, since nearly all of the foods you buy will be nonperishable, you can begin hunting for hard-to-find items months in advance, if you wish. Look for packaged dinners requiring that you add meat and, instead, plan to add an envelope of meat-flavored vegetable protein bits (beef, chicken, ham). Powdered non-fat dry milk and powdered eggs and egg substitutes are universally available. Don't overlook the health food store. Since they serve many vegetarian customers, they often have good selections of dry, lightweight meat substitute products. On our last trip, we tried a "burger" product from the health food store made of soy and sesame. It was so good, I'll be buying some to eat at home.

Tuna, or any canned fish or meat, can be alternated with the vegetable protein, especially if weight is not a serious factor. When bringing canned goods along, the cans must be carried out of the woods as well as in. For that reason, hard salami may be a better choice of meat to add to some of your dinners. It keeps without refrigeration, and tastes especially good in meals like spaghetti or noodles with cheese sauce.

Sauce mixes are good bases for meal planning—with pasta, quick-cooking rice, or a dry potato mix (hash brown, scalloped) and vegetable or meat protein added. Be careful about relying entirely upon vegetable protein, unless you are well versed in vegetarian eating habits. Ounce for ounce the soy-protein meat substitutes do not satisfy the body's need for protein as animal protein does. Natural cheese keeps up to two weeks, especially those kinds which are packaged wrapped in wax, such as gouda. If you are bringing some cans, and if you want to splurge on one rather heavy meal, a canned ham cooked on a campfire is a real treat. All you have to do is loosen the lid of the can and with the key provided, place it by the coals and let it simmer in its own juices for about a half hour, or until it smells too good to wait any longer.

Of course, if you are back packing, or if you are taking a canoe trip with long portages, you will want to avoid cans and reduce the weight and bulk of your food pack as much as possible. Planning for this purpose can be an adventure in itself. On one canoe trip we took that required as many as 8 portages per day, my husband thought up a unique idea. Noticing how much space flake-type cereal takes in a package, he decided to reduce it by pulverizing it in the blender. The whole family got rather carried away, throwing every kind of cereal we had in the cupboard into the blender until we had a whole pile of what looked like sawdust. Although hardly aesthetically appealing, we were all game to give it a try. The resulting breakfast food took up less than a quarter of the space of the original flakes. Rehydrated with milk and served with raisins, it proved to be quite palatable. Served with stewed prunes it was even enjoyable. Believe it or not, we ate this for breakfast every day for 2 weeks. By the end of that time, it was as regular a part of my morning routine as my first cup of coffee.

On the other hand, if you are bicycling or skiing between inns where its easy to reprovision, your family can pretty much eat as you all choose. But just think of all the fun of martyrdom you'll be missing!

A snack is a welcome pick-me-up for mid-morning and afternoon breaks, especially if you're working hard or if the weather is cool or wet, and you need some recharging with glucose. Dried fruits are good plain or rehydrated, for desserts or just for munching, and they help provide necessary vitamins. The gorp mixture mentioned in the menu is a good quick-energy snack which helps to round out a light lunch. In fact, I know some people who eat only gorp for lunch. The only problem with this food is that it may not be appropriate for some of the youngest members of the party, since it has nuts and M&M's which might make you fear choking. For this reason, the recipe was reluctantly retired from our repertoire for a couple of years, until we thought our children could handle it. We like to include a few evening snacks such as popcorn or marshmallows for toasting, should we have a campfire.

You will probably want to keep your family's tastes in mind, but I like to experiment a bit, more so than at home. We all work up enough of an appetite so that we're much less fussy than

we are at home. And, if your efforts on your first trip aren't as successful as you'd wished, don't despair. Your wilderness cooking will improve as you make little discoveries about what to use and how to use it. For example, instant pudding mixed thoroughly several hours ahead and left to set until serving time can match pudding made at home. But the first few times we made it camping, we mixed it just before mealtime and ended up with a lumpy, runny mess. Similarly, the ground beef convenience dinners (supplemented with soy protein) we suffered through for several seasons, improved vastly when I started leaving out the "*seasoning packet*" and adding my own simple seasoning.

Fire

Whether you decide to cook on a stove or a fire will depend upon where you are camping, your own preferences, and a number of other factors. Be sure to follow all local fire regulations. They vary greatly from one area to another across the country. In many high-use areas fires are completely forbidden. In almost any area that is under state or federal control, a dry season can bring about bans on campfires. And in many privately-owned areas, such as the forest areas owned by the lumber companies of Maine, fires are permitted only at authorized campsites. If you are camping at a site that is not authorized in any area, whether very remote or highly used, it is important to leave no trace of your visit, and no sign of your having used a fire if indeed you have built one.

Forestry people suggest building a fire on a rock base covered with dirt, then dismantling this setup before leaving camp. In this way, a ring of soot-covered rocks doesn't mar the side of the trail. When we camp in a highly used area, or in any area which does not have established campsites, we usually make it a point to refrain from using a fire. This way we disturb the ecology as little as possible. I find this a good educational experience for the children, and not really much of an inconvenience for us. Sitting around a campfire has a great aesthetic value, but the beauty of the unspoiled woods is better.

If you will be using a fire—and I don't mean to be down on campfires; in many areas they are perfectly justified—a biscuit mix is a good staple to include in your food pack. If you're bringing a Dutch oven or reflector baker, there are many tasty treats you can whip up with it. But a good breakfast or dessert bread can be made over the fire with no oven or pans at all. I'll call them "Jam Dandies" since I was first introduced to them that way at Girl Scout camp.

Jam Dandies

Find several medium-stout (about 34 inch) green sticks and clean off an area about four inches long at one end of each. Mix two cups biscuit mix (the commercial type with shortening and leavening already added) add ⅓ cup water. Divide into six parts and mold each into a long "snake." Kids love to help with this part, if you can stand it! Coil tightly around the cleaned end of the stick and toast until browned and done. Slide off the stick and fill the center with jam, jelly or honey. These are very messy but delicious.

On a day when you're moving camp and want an early start, you can't beat granola for a filling and nutritious breakfast. Many people also like to use it as a trail snack. I find the commercially available types too sweet and quite expensive, so I make my own.

Granola

12 cups old-fashioned (not quick cooking) rolled oats
1 cup wheat germ
4 Tablespoons brown sugar
1 cup chopped almonds
¾ cup honey
⅔ cup corn or safflower oil
1 tablespoon vanilla
1 cup raisins and/or dates

Mix dry ingredients, then add honey and stir until coated. Combine oil and vanilla and stir into cereal mixture. Spread in two shallow baking pans and bake at 325° for about a half hour, or until browned to your taste. After the granola has cooled, break it into pieces and add the dried fruit of your choice.

Spaghetti Dinner (6 servings)

1 1-lb whole-wheat or enriched spaghetti
1 1-lb "hard" salami, peeled and diced
1 5-oz. can tomato paste
*2 tablespoons instant minced onion
*Italian seasoning, according to taste
*can be mixed together in a small plastic pag before leaving home.

Boil the spaghetti according to package directions. Drain and set aside. Mix tomato paste, salami seasonings, onion and 3 cans water. Bring to a boil. Add cooked spaghetti and heat thoroughly. It's ready to serve.

The following recipe can be even more simplified by using a convenience "fried rice" flavored instant rice mix in place of the soup mix and instant rice.

Fried Rice (6 servings)

Make a small omelet from dehydrated eggs, cut into bit-size pieces and set aside.
In a large pot, mix together and bring to boil:
3 tablespoons margarine
1 envelope onion soup mix
2 cups water

Stir in 2 cups instant rice and reserved omelet. Remove from stove, cover, and allow to sit for about 7 minutes. Before serving, stir once with fork.

A hearty meal to enjoy on a "rest day," at a site where a campfire is a good idea.

Lentil Stew

Early in the day, or even the night before, pour boiling water to a depth of at least 2 inches over—
1 cup lentils
About 1 hour and 15 minutes before supertime, drain the lentils and add
6–8 cups water
1 package soup-making mix (the kind to which you're supposed to add meat)

Bring to a boil, boil 5 minutes, then set to simmer at the side of the fireplace until the lentils are soft.

Fresh vegetables can certainly be included in your pack. We generally bring some fresh carrots along since they keep well, and are enjoyable either cooked or raw. Potatoes and celery are also good to bring along. Firm, fresh fruits such as apples can also be included on your menus. Care should be taken in packing these and all items, however, in order to keep them in the best possible condition.

What we've found to be the most convenient and organized way to pack foods for camping is to prepackage each meal in its own separate plastic bag. By eliminating the store packages, you save space. By packing each meal separately rather than in bulk, you are able to waterproof each meal individually. You can easily prove, while packing, that you've brought the correct amounts to last throughout your trip, and you eliminate the endless shuffling through the pack each time a meal is prepared. There are a few items we keep in bulk form, such as staples like coffee, sugar, salt. Items such as fresh fruit and vegetables get special treatment, but everything else sets sealed away. Fresh produce rots quickly if it is sealed in a plastic bag with no refrigeration. I keep mine in a porous bag at the top of the food pack. The staple items in plastic containers fill out the pack's pockets.

Most of the time I now use the self-sealing kind of plastic bags available at the supermarket which have a zipper type of closure. But sometimes these are not easily found in the needed sizes, at least not in my area. No problem—I simply revert to the old sealing method I used before the zipper bags were introduced. To seal a conventional plastic bag, I use a straw, some aluminum foil, and an iron. First I lay a strip of foil on the ironing board, fill the bag, then lay the bag with the open end on top of the strip of foil. Closing the bag most of the way, I squeeze as much air out of it with my hands as I can. I put the straw through the opening I've allowed, and suck out as much of the remaining air as possible. Then, laying a second strip of foil on top of the open end of the bag, I press the iron on top of the foil for several seconds. I check the seal and, if necessary, heat it again for a few seconds longer. It is important to eliminate as much air as possible and to seal the bag as close to its contents as possible in order to keep the food freshest.

Sealing food bags under supervision.

Packing and sealing meals for a trip of a week or two week's duration can be quite a job, but it is time well spent. Once you're out in the woods, you will have to spend a minimum amount of time and energy dealing with food preparation if you have planned and packaged this way, and there are other advantages as well. Animals will be less attracted to your food pack if everything is neatly sealed up in plastic. Should you set out for a day trip from your campsite, your lunch will be already packed—you packed it before you left home. If you can enlist the help of spouse and children in the packing activity, you can set up a mini-assembly line and get the work done in no time at all.

But foods don't have to be all convenience on your camping trip. After all, they should be fun. To add a little interest and a lot of nutrition to your diet, you could encouarge your children to grow a vegetable garden in their packs. Mung beans, alfalfa and cress are easily grown in plastic bags inside the pockets of packs adding very little weight. And the fun of seeing them grow will add to the enjoyment of the trip. Rinse the seeds with water once each day, and a healthy crop should be ready in three to five days.

Another food source which is particularly interesting to older children, and to many adults, too, is the woods themselves. There are many fine guidebooks on wild foods to help you choose some tasty edibles from the environment surrounding you. It might be interesting to try to live off the land for one full day. Or, you might try to collect some different leaves for brewing different teas and compare which concoctions taste best. Be sure you know what you're eating, for there are many poisonous plants in the woods and fields. And young children like my two toddlers (by now they're called "pre-schoolers") are forbidden to eat **anything,** even a blueberry, without an OK from an adult in our party. With proper supervision, though, the two of them are among the most avid collectors of fiddleheads and blackberries I've seen. It's a good way to add fresh food to your diet, and it's very satisfying to find your own food in a new environment.

So, bon appetit! With some planning, some time, and some imagination, you'll be devising meals that will be light, compact, nutritious, easy, affordable, fun—and tasty.

5. THE BACKPACKING FAMILY

For the family whose children are old enough to walk a reasonable distance and can carry at least their own clothing or sleeping bags on their backs, backpacking is the logical way to explore the wilderness. It requires somewhat less of an investment in equipment and the simplest form of locomotion—walking—rather than having to learn to ski, paddle, or ride a bike. You won't have to travel far from home, either. Extensive hiking trails exist in virtually very part of our country. Camping techniques for backpackers also apply to winter campers, canoers, and bicycle campers.

Some specialized equipment is necessary for an enjoyable backpacking holiday, but this equipment has its own advantages. First, it can be used for other forms of wilderness camping. Your pack and frame could be useful on a canoe or ski touring trip as well as on a hiking trip. And, if you rent equipment for your first few times out, the rental fee for backpacking equipment is generally lower than for the gear required for other types of camping.

Where do you start? First, to your friendly outfitter. Oh, it's certainly wise to read up on the subject before you get there to learn something about the relative merits of different materials and structures. But books and magazines can't give you as good an idea of what you want as shopping around can. Also, many of the better camping stores have personnel working in them who are extremely well informed and helpful, since most of them are active in the outdoors and have personally tested much of the equipment they sell.

What should you know before you get there? First of all, that the most important piece of gear you need is some footwear that will allow you to walk long distances over different types of terrain with a pack on your back. If you bought a good pair of hiking boots before you began your daytripping, you're probably all set. If not, don't expect your sneakers to suffice on an extended backpacking trip. They simply won't hold up.

Boots needed for most backpacking trips are referred to as lightweight or medium weight hiking boots by most of the dealers and manufacturers. Heavyweight and rock-climbing boots are made for more specialized activities, and are not appropriate for regular backpacking. The fit of the boot is the most important aspect of all. A boot which does not fit properly can cause all kinds of problems on even simple hikes. The best way to get properly fitted is to go to a reputable dealer and be measured and fitted professionally. If it is not possible for you to get to a store which sells this type of equipment, some of the best mail order houses who handle mountaineering equipment do sell boots by mail and require that you send a foot outline. If you order boots by mail, check them for fit immediately. Shuffle your feet back and forth to make sure that your toes do not touch the front tip of the boot. Wear them around the house for increasing lengths of time to test for comfort. If you are satisfied that the fit is correct, then wear the boots outside. It will take a while to "break in" any pair of boots, but watch out for any real discomfort, especially when your boots are brand new.

You should wear a fairly heavy wool sock with your boots. I generally wear a "ragg" sock. Many people are irritated by wool, and they may want to wear a nylon or cotton liner sock between their skin and the wool sock. These are recommended as standard by many people who feel that the combination of the two types of socks helps to protect the feet from blisters. You will need several pairs of these, for it is necessary on long hikes to change socks often.

Just as you found your day pack helped carry a day's load a lot more comfortably, a pack and packframe carry the load required for a longer trip in the most comfortable manner. These frames are constructed of tubular aluminum or manganese and are designed to hold the weight so that it is carried mostly on your hips. This allows you a straighter posture that is more comfortable on longer hikes. The pack and frame are held on to your body by straps at the shoulder and by a waist strap, which may have to be purchased separately. When these straps are adjusted properly, and they should be pulled tight, your load is easily carried. If they are not adjusted correctly, or if the waist belt is missing, the packer's comfort is very much affected. Again, the reputable dealer is invaluable in helping you to select and understand the equipment you need.

There are many manufacturers of packs, and each produces at least several models. The pack you choose will depend largely upon personal preference. I personally like the undivided pack. My pack is simply one big cavity of coated nylon with four pockets on the outside of it. Packs are available with all sorts of zippered compartments, and many people find the multi compartmented packs the most efficient. With the compartmented system, one may have designated spots for the sleeping bag, the clothing, the mess kit. The reason I prefer the undivided version is that my family's needs change, our interests change, and what we bring along on our camping trips changes. Sometimes we bring a camera and sometimes we don't. A while back I would have filled a compartment with diapers, and now we don't have to bring any. So that's why I like my undivided pack. It's versatile. And I don't have to worry about having an odd-sized mess kit fitting into a compartment. It may take a bit of arranging and rearranging, but somehow I'm going to be able to fit it into that one big cavity, my pack.

Your children may or may not be old enough for a pack and frame. If they are young, they may enjoy carrying their clothes in a child-size rucksack. Or, they may carry their own sleeping bags or sleeping bag straps. These are a set of straps which go around a sleeping bag stuffed into a sack and loop around the child's shoulders forming a pack-type arrangement.

The main problem for the backpacking parent of a very young child is that of transporting both the camping gear and the child. While there are several fine baby carriers or "kiddy packs" on the market, the parent can't carry much gear at the same time. If one parent must carry a child, the other parent and any older brothers or sisters available must carry all the gear. Luckily, there are several ways one might try to cope with this dilemma, although some may seem a bit strange at first glance!

First, you can make a real effort to reduce your gear to the barest minimum of bulk and weight. You may be able to do without a tent if you will be in an area where Adirondack or other type of shelters are available. A lightweight nylon fly may be substituted for a tent if you travel out of bug season. If you can afford it, you can rely on freeze-dried foods and cut down on the weight of food and cooking utensils. You will also be able to cut down on fuel. When choosing stoves, keep this problem in mind.

Toddlers should be encouraged to walk rather than be carried. Put them "in training" in advance for your trip, by taking them for walks of increasing length and you can help them build up their stamina. Tiny rucksacks can be bought or made so that even the toddler can carry a small amount of lightweight gear. As long as they are not pushed beyond their physical limits, they will probably enjoy the trip all the more for being included this way in the activity.

If you have a dog, even he can carry a pack. Again, you can find your wilderness camping store a help—you can ask them to show you the latest in "doggie packs." I've never tried one of these with my dog. Being a great water lover, he'd undoubtedly soak anything I put in a pack on his back. Or else he might drown under the weight of it. But I know several people whose dogs do use these packs and, if your dog is appropriate in size and temperament, this might be a solution. If the price of the pack is prohibitive, analyze the construction and you may be able to make one at home.

With a second family you may be able to divide community gear such as cooking utensils, stove, first-aid kit and saw between the packs of two different families. This can go a long way towards making room in your pack for all the things you need to bring, and you'll like the added companionship.

If all these suggestions don't work, you're not alone. Since our daughters were born just a little over a year apart, we were faced with the prospect of carrying both that first year. Don't give up—I have one last resort, one final suggestion. You can hike into a wilderness location for a base camp, a minimum distance from the car. Once there, one parent can stay with the children while the other makes the trip back for a pack full of gear. The second parent may also have to take a turn for a return trip. From this base camp, you can take day hikes, returning to camp at night. While this sounds less adventurous, it can be quite a lot of fun in a location carefully chosen with this type of trip in mind.

Whichever way you go, I suggest you be conservative in the terrain you choose to explore. Remember, you will either have a hiking toddler for whom the easiest terrain will be a challenge, or you will be carrying a youngster on your back. You will want to be extremely careful that you don't fall yourself. If you try to cover too much ground in one day, you may have some unhappy little people on your hands. Children's attention spans are short, and they can get bored and irritable after a few hours. Their physical stamina is not great, so for both of these reasons it helps to take rest stops often, sometimes accompanied by a snack or a drink, especially in hot weather.

If you take your time, take it easy, stop to look at the flowers, as they say, you'll probably all be looking forward to your next trip before you're even back home.

6. FAMILY SKI TOURING

So you've been on a few backpacking trips and have grown to like it? You don't have to put those day packs away for the winter, you know. The woods are just as pretty then, in some ways even prettier. A covering of snow gives the woods a feeling of quiet and peace that is matched nowhere. And the absence of leaves make the most of distant views from overlooks on snowy hillsides. Animal tracks are easily spotted and recognized after a fresh layer of snow has covered the forest floor.

You can take to snowshoes, but for a really exhilarating experience, and for a sport which can last a lifetime for you and your children, you can try ski touring. This sport, which has recently soared in popularity in the United States, has been familiar to Europeans for centuries. If you watched the cross-country ski races of the winter Olympics on television, you may have a picture of this type of skiing as very demanding and exhausting, requiring a high degree of physical fitness and skill. While this is true of cross-country ski racing—probably one of the most grueling and painful of individual sports competition—ski touring is an entirely different pastime.

Ski touring, as the name suggests, allows you to take your time and look around. It is non-competitive. While acquiring a certain degree of skill and form can add to the pleasure of the sport, you needn't be an olympic racer to participate. Beginners can have a great time. The skills involved are easily acquired. But the best feature of the sport (and I really think this is one of **the** best sports) is that just about anyone can do it—young or old, big or small, strong or weak. It's a sport you can take part in from early childhood until old age, at your own pace. In an age of Little League and Pop Warner, I think it's important for children to be exposed to lifetime sports—those that they can still enjoy after school graduation, or if they don't make the team. This is one such sport, and one to which you may introduce your children with a limited amount of effort and expense.

The Alpine skier will be pleasantly surprised when he shops for cross-country equipment for the first time. A complete outfit can be obtained for a hundred dollars, although prices range to well above that figure. By complete outfit, I refer to boots, skis, bindings and poles.

Some people who have Alpine equipment try to adapt it to cross-country skiing, so they can see if they like the sport before they invest money in equipment. I wonder how many people are turned away from cross-country skiing each year by this practice? The answer must be at least in the thousands. If you want to try it before you buy any equipment, good for you. That certainly makes a lot of sense to me. But, you can't get any valid idea of what ski touring is like by trying it with heavy, cumbersome downhill equipment. It would be like trying to swim wearing hiking boots. If you want to give ski touring a try, be fair to the sport—use the correct equipment.

There are many areas blossoming across the country—more each year as the sport gains in popularity, where you can rent equipment for a reasonable price. While some areas charge trail fees, the fee for trail maintenance is usually only about five dollars (unlike downhill ski areas where the fee is near $20), so the cost of renting equipment and skiing at a x-c ski center shouldn't be prohibitive, even for the whole family. One area near our home, where we often ski with the children, charges no fee, but accepts donations of any amount toward trail upkeep. Equipment can be rented there for $5.00 per half day. And this includes everything you'll need—skis, boots and poles.

Clothing should be much lighter than you'd need for downhill skiing. Since ski touring involves more constant activity, that down parka you might wear Alpine skiing will probably be too restrictive and just plain too hot to wear skiing cross-country. Again, the layered approach to dressing is probably the best, since it allows you a greater number of options. The traditional outfit for cross-country skiing is knickers, but a pair of jeans will do just fine, as long as they're not too tight fitting. As in hiking, most people recommend a two-sock system, a light nylon or cotton sock topped by a heavier one of wool, to be worn under ski boots. Again, I usually just wear one wool sock on each foot. For the upper body, a turtleneck, a wool shirt or sweater, a down or synthetic-filled vest and a windbreaker can be worn in any combination which dictates comfort as the day progresses. You will probably wear a fairly light combination while skiing, unless it is very cold, but will want to add a sweater or vest if you stop for a break. The windbreaker is important, as it can make the difference between being cold and being comfortable on a windy day. A wool ski hat which covers the ears is important. Your hat should be the first to go on when you get cold, and the first to come off as you overheat. You won't feel out of place in any outfit you devise. Comfort is what's important here.

When it comes time to buy equipment, you will find a great selection, quite different from when I bought my first skis twelve years ago. At that time, Scandinavian wood skis were all that was available. Now, wood and synthetic skis, waxless and requiring wax, are made in many European countries and in the United States. The best skis for you will depend a great deal on your abilities and preferences, and on how you intend to use the skis. When I bought my first pair of skis, we went to John Caldwell's shop in Vermont and asked his advice. Since I had virtually no skiing experience, downhill or otherwise, except for a couple of afternoons skiing on borrowed cross-country skis, he recommended a fairly wide pair of strong, quality wood skis. They were a good pair of learning skis, and I used them until a few years ago when I replaced them with some narrower fiberglass ones. While many people reject wood because they feel it won't hold up, my skis were in good enough condition after seven years of hard use so that I could sell them.

Many people shy away from waxable skis because the waxing process itself appears complicated. High performance waxing can be very involved and painstaking, but the recreational skier can enjoy x-c skiing through a simplified waxing system. Most of the major ski wax companies now market a two-wax system for wet and dry snow. The easiest way to test which of these two waxes to use is by using a simple snowball test. Send the kids out in the yard to make snowballs. Or, better yet, a snowman. If they soon return to the house saying that the snow won't form balls, then the dry wax is the wax of the day. If, on the other hand, the yard is decorated with snowmen and a snowfort or two by the time you've finished the breakfast dishes, the wet wax is the one to use. These two waxes will suffice under most conditions; you will need at least two additional waxes—probably a blue klister and a silver klister—for icy and extremely wet conditions.

While the two harder waxes are fairly easy to apply (you just crayon them onto the bottom surface of the sky), applying a klister is more complicated. These are softer waxes that are sold in tubes. Apply sparingly in dots along the length of the ski, and then spread evenly. This is much easier to do if the klister is warm.

If it is cold, you may have to soften it by applying a torch to the tube until it is soft enough. It's easier, though, to just prevent the waxes from becoming too cold in the first place. Keep them indoors, and carry them in an inside pocket close to your body when on the trail.

Every convert to waxless skis has at least one horror story to tell about getting stuck on the trail with the wrong wax, and either not being able to climb, or having chunks of snow frozen to the wax on the botton of his skis. However, there's really no excuse for such problems. Bring along a scraper to remove a problem wax along with some other waxes to use if conditions change during a tour. You should never have severe wax problems.

Waxless skis have come a long way, however, and their convenience, especially for the skiing family, is undebated. These skis need no waxing. Some use a structural modification in the ski itself to allow the skier to climb up hills more easily but still glide down. These modifications differ according to the manufacturer. Trak's NO-WAX® skis employ a modified scale-type design on the plastic cki bottom. Other brands use strips of mohair, grooved designs or other means of providing friction at the critical part of the ski under the foot, which touches the snow while the skier climbs, but is above the surface of the ground while gliding.

It is important to shop for good quality waxless skis, and to make sure of proper fit. This is more critical in the case of waxless skis than their waxable counterparts. Several of my friends purchased "bargain" waxless skis a few years ago. They soon found themselves stuck with real "lemons", mistakenly manufactured with too long a mohair strip. Climbing was fine, until they found they had to climb downhill, too! Similarly, I have suffered through an afternoon of trying to encourage a youngster whose parents had bought her a pair of waxless skis in a "grow into" size. Since she was too small to weigh down the part of the ski under her foot, she was unable to walk up even gentle hills, and had to spend a large part of the tour side-stepping.

As in the case of purchasing other equipment, the knowledgeable dealer should be consulted when you are buying ski touring equipment. It is far better to pay more money and buy a

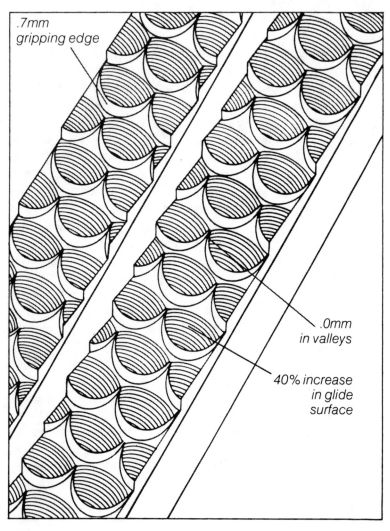

.7mm
gripping edge

.0mm
in valleys

40% increase
in glide
surface

This is a drawing of the Trak® Fishscale™ Nowax® base. This convex fishscale pattern improves glide as well as kick and climbing ability.

product from someone who knows about what he or she is selling, than to "bargain hunt" and end up with equipment that is either unusable, or just plain unenjoyable.

Whether you buy waxless skis or use a simplified waxing system, I think it's wise to encourage your child to care for his or her own equipment at as young an age as possible. This practice not only preserves the equipment, but also takes the mystery out of it. Treat the cross-country skis as you would a prized toy or a bicycle, and you may find your child ski-touring in the yard after school. Certainly a much healthier activity than playing video games or just watching television!

Choosing a ski is a very personal matter. Some people prefer wood because it's traditional, or for any number of reasons; some people prefer fiberglass because they feel it holds up better. I chose fiberglass simply because at the time I could get a better deal on a quality pair of fiberglass skis than I could find on a comparable pair of wood. But, except for that consideration, I had not ruled out a pair of good wooden light touring skis by the same manufacturer who made my first pair. Some people are frightened off by the prospect of waxing skis, and for those people the waxless ski is probably a wise choice.

Good skis are made of different materials; they are also made in a variety of widths. For the beginner, it's important that the ski not be too narrow. The very narrow skis are intended mainly for racing and are difficult to use for the beginner. They are also nearly impossible to use with a pack on your back. So, if you are thinking of doing any camping on your skis, I think a moderate width, about 55 millimeters wide, is a good choice. Some instructors use a "graduated width method" to teach beginners how to cross-country ski. They start them on a pair of 65 millimeters skis, progress to 56 millimeters, and graduate them to a 50 millimeter light touring ski. If you do not intend to camp on skis and would like to own a pair of narrow, light touring skis, perhaps it would be a good idea to get a little practice on rented skis of moderate width before you buy your own narrower skis.

Skis for children are another matter. Since the skis will not last a great number of seasons anyway, because of size changes, durability is probably not a critical factor in choosing skis for young children, unless they are particularly reckless or destruction-prone. For the same reason, you may not want to pay a great deal of money for skis which can only be used a short time. Some of the manufacturers seem to take these factors into consideration and put out some very economical children's ski outfits. Our daughters both have the same kind of ski outfit, Scandinavian wood and fiberglass skis, poles and cable bindings, which cost us about twelve dollars for the whole package. Next time around we expect to have to pay more, due to inflation and to the added cost of larger sizes, but hope to still be able to equip them for a modest sum. For the school-age child who is apt to want to run out and ski afternoons after school, I think a pair of waxless skis would be a good choice, since it would allow the child more time skiing, and wouldn't scare him off as several afternoons of skiing on the wrong choice of wax might.

Next is the question of boots. It is possible to ski in a pair of light hiking boots attached to the ski with a cable-type cross-country binding. For young children, I think this is the way to go, for reasons of cost and stability. Hiking boots are more versatile, and probably can be acquired for less money. For older children who are beginning to master the sport, and for adults, I think the cross-country ski boot is preferable. It allows you to achieve greater performance, and is undoubtedly more comfortable to ski in than the hiking boot-cable combination.

The binding, which holds only the tip of the boot to the ski, allowing all but the toes of the feet to the raised, is devised of either three or four "pins," metal posts which fit into corresponding holes on the sole of the boot. A clamp, which fits over the top of the boot sole around the toe area, holds them tight. Some people prefer bindings which also have a cable going around the back of the boot, but most people opt just for the toe binding.

Poles are made of bamboo, fiberglass, or aluminum. Bamboo poles are the least expensive. They don't last as long as fiberglass or aluminum; so the price/durability factor seems to even out. The technique of sitting down on your poles or using your poles as a brake on steep descents will wear out a pair of bamboo poles very quickly. The newer fiberglass poles have a "clam digger" basket, which doesn't get caught as easily on underbrush. Be sure to teach your kids to keep their poles "in" when cruising downhill. Alpine ski poles can be used in a pinch. Just remember that weight and cumbersomeness are factors to be considered. Also, make sure that the straps around the gloves are tightened sufficiently.

Waxing has sometimes been made out to be such a mystique that it has frightened many people away. At one area where we skied once this past winter, people were paying money for a professional "wax job" just to avoid choosing and applying their own wax. It really is not anywhere near as complicated as some people make it appear. Most of the wax companies distribute charts, and many dealers produce charts which encompass all the brands of wax they sell. These make it easy to choose the right wax for the temperature and type of snow you encounter. The right wax makes skiing a real joy, enabling you to walk right up very steep trails and glide down the hills on the other side, giving you good "kick" off of one ski and allowing you to glide a maximum distance on the other.

Consult a chart and you should be able to make a reasonable choice of wax. It is best to choose a wax on the cold side when in doubt, since the waxes for colder conditions are harder than those for warmer conditions, and the soft, warm waxes tend to freeze if they're used when it is too cold for them. A torch aids in softening the wax so it can be spread evenly along the ski. If you rent skis at an area, you may want to hang around and watch the wax being applied, so you will have a good idea of how to do it when you get your own skis. Waxing is not difficult, and there are many books and magazine articles which deal extensively with the subject. Don't forget that a pine tar base must be torched onto wooden skis to enable them to hold the wax better.

The technique of cross-country skiing probably resembles skating more than anything else. You'll notice that the skis don't have metal edges like alpine skis. This gives you more lateral mobility. While poling yourself forward, give a slight kick with one foot and glide forward with the other. This propelling push for-

The first step in cross-country skiing. Maintain your balance, feel comfortable, and lift up your heels. Note the cable bindings on the child's skis for greater stability.

Coasting down a gentle incline teaches proper balance. It's fun, too!

Learning proper glide technique is a matter of practice. This child is having difficulty because her poles are too high for her (poles should come up only to your armpits). I bet those alpine poles belong to her mother.

Kids can learn to climb by scrambling up small hills on their own. Even though this child is not gripping her poles properly, her weight is well distributed over her front ski. If the hill is too steep, they can always use the herringbone technique, or side-step. In a bind, they can always take their skis off.

This little fellow is practicing an advanced telemark technique, which enables you to get down over your skis for better stability and turning. This is an excellent technique for deep snow. His poles are well out of the snow in anticipation.

ward is finished by almost throwing the pole out behind you (hence the tight strap). Meanwhile, you are swinging your other pole hand out in front of you, ready for the next pole plant and gliding step. Be sure not to point the pole in front of you. Your hand will be well in front of your pole plant, which will be near your forward foot. With practice you will pick up your heels and develop an easy, natural gliding motion. Remember that the secret to happy ski-touring is not wasting any motion.

You will find that you can glide up gentle hills and scamper or "tip-toe" up others. Only the very steepest and slickest sections will have to be done in the herringbone or side-step fashion. There is nothing wrong with taking off your skis and climbing up the steepest, slickest slopes—especially if a skier comes barrelling down towards you, and you have to dive into the woods.

Skiing downhill on cross-country skis requires balance. The alpine "egg" position will get you down the hill the quickest. To slow down and turn requires mastery of the snowplow technique. A more advanced way to turn on steep hills is the telemark technique, which lowers your center of gravity for stability and works well in deep snow. The easiest turn on the flat is the simple step turn. And whatever is simplest in cross-country is always the best.

Where can you take your family to ski? That's the joy of it—**ANYWHERE!** The state park where you used to hike on day trips might be a good choice, or perhaps the local golf course, a friend's farm, or your own back yard. Anyplace you're allowed to go that offers terrain and scenery to suit your interests is fair game. On weekends, we often go to one of the two state forests near our town (we're lucky) or travel a little farther to find interesting, new terrain. On weekday afternoons, we ski behind our house on a series of trails which crosses parts of several properties. Since most people don't use their yards much in mid-winter, and since skiing is a quiet sport as opposed to such outings as snowmobiling, most people don't mind you being there as long as you don't go close to the house. You can ask and receive permission to ski in any number of places. Even if you live in the city, there are usually parks, golf courses and cemeteries where you may be able to ski. It costs nothing, and the pleasure is unlimited.

Ski touring areas, while they often charge a small amount of money for their use, are enjoyable places to go now and then. On a cold day, a hot cup of coffee or soup served at the warming hut makes the day a lot more enjoyable. If you have small children along, one parent can switch off with the other and stay around the practice area and warming hut with the children while the other parent skis the trails of his choice. We often do this and find it has an added bonus: our daughters developed a greater interest in the sport when they found that other people enjoy this activity. It wasn't just some kind of aberration on their parents' part! Being the smallest skiers we encountered one year, they loved all the attention they received from the other skiers, and tried to ski all the harder to show off. While I'm not sure I approve of the motive, at least their skiing improved! By the end of the season, our three-year old could easily ski around the 2.5 kilometer beginners loop, and even the two-year old made it around on one occasion.

The ski area with a warming hut is also a good way for the family which includes a baby to be able to ski. Parents again could take turns skiing and staying with baby at the hut. When our girls were very tiny, we skied with them on our backs in kiddy packs. As long as you're careful about controlling your speed, and as long as you save the more challenging terrain for days when you're alone and baby stays home, this is a safe practice. Remember that when you are skiing with a child on your back, while you may be feeling perfectly warm, the child is not exercising and may be a lot colder than you are. It's wise to check often, and bring plenty of warm clothes for burdling him up. A pair of adult's wool socks over the baby's boots can really help keep those little feet warm. On very cold days, though, it is best for the baby to stay at home or in the warming hut.

How do you teach your toddlers to ski? You don't. At least, I have found non-teaching to be the best way to introduce them to the sport. They can begin by just shuffling along. Even early walkers can accomplish this. In fact, the son of one of my former neighbors started skiing before he mastered walking, using the poles for support. Since children are born imitators, they will pick up the technique as they go along, just by watching you and other adults. Once in a while you may want to give the child a little pointer, but most of the time they will make fine progress with very little direction from you. And, especially if you start your little ones at a very young age, their physical coordination may not permit them to go beyond the shuffling stage that first season. To try to get them to do what they are physically not ready to do may frustrate them to the point that they will lose interest. By just letting things happen and having a good time, you will probably encourage better skiing in future years.

As your family gets more grown up, you may want to try camping on skis. You may tent if your equipment is suited for the low temperatures and other conditions of winter camping, or you may stay in cabins or hostels instead. There are many areas where this is possible. Local guidebooks on areas for cross-country skiing can help you locate such places. Magazines and other periodicals relating to the sport of cross-country skiing also may have articles or advertisements which can give you ideas for places to go. If you want an extended ski trip, but don't want to camp out, there are some places where trail networks are laid out so that you can ski from inn to inn. One such place is the town of Jackson, New Hampshire, where there is a vast network of trails spanning all ranges of difficulty which join various inns, hotels, and public buildings all over the town. The town even provides a shuttle bus to take skiers from their destinations back to their cars.

If there seem to be limitless opportunities for cross-country skiing, it's true. One can spend as much or as little time at it as he wishes. You can choose to master challenging terrain, or just putter. Whichever way, it's a sport with a level of enjoyment and aesthetic appeal that's hard to match. And a sport which, if terrain is chosen to match physical condition and skiing ability, your child can enjoy all his life.

7. CANOE CAMPING

Probably the most pleasing way to explore the wilderness, and probably the easiest, is by canoe. While it requires more involved equipment than some of the other forms of camping, locating a canoe, paddles, and life preservers, it is an easy way for a family, especially one with young children who cannot walk a great distance, to penetrate the wilderness. Canoe camping is what I recommend for the ultimate wilderness experience with children. There are unlimited opportunities for good, safe trips in beautiful surroundings, and it's a pleasant way to transport yourselves, your children and your gear with minimum effort. Once you've become accustomed to it, paddling even a fully loaded canoe becomes automatic and nearly effortless.

What type of canoe to choose is as personal a matter as which set of cross-country skis. If I were to buy a new canoe today, I'd have to do a lot of shopping around to find the one that would best suit my interests. There is no right canoe for everyone. What each family must do is to sit down and think about what they want to do with their canoe before they look into different brands, materials and constructions. Will your travel be restricted to lake camping? Or, will you also want a boat suitable for whitewater? If you will be using it on whitewater, will the rivers be mostly the big, heavy rivers characteristic of the West, or the smaller, ledgy rivers of the Northeast? Will you be fishing from your canoe? How much use is the boat likely to get, and how sturdy must it be? And, lastly, how much can you afford to spend?

There are some general principles that you should keep in mind when seeking out the right canoe for your purposes. Length is obviously important. This depends upon the average size of the group you would take on most trips and the length of the trip (supplies). If most of your paddling will be on lakes and open bodies of water, you will want a canoe with a wide middle and a keel. Although aluminum canoes are the lightest and easiest to carry, remember that they can be blown about a lot more easily too. You can run into a lot of wind on open water.

After you determine where you want to use your canoe and for what purposes, you will find, when you begin to shop around, that canoes are made of basically five materials, and that each material has inherent advantages and disadvantages.

1. Wood and Canvas

This is the traditional combination of materials from which canoes were made for many years. Some traditionalists still prefer them. They are aesthetically pleasing, having a natural wood interior, and cruise quietly through the water.

The main drawback of this type of canoe is that the materials tend to soak up water. On a trip, this can mean that your canoe may gain weight as your trip progresses. If the boat is not properly maintained, this can lead to rotting of the wooden structure. Maintenance involves keeping the canvas intact and sealed, and varnishing the interior about once annually. Other canoe materials require no special maintenance unless there is damage to be repaired.

Some people feel that the likelihood of damaging a wood and canvas boat on a rocky stretch of river is greater than that of damaging a canoe made of other materials. In any case, rips and punctures must be promptly repaired in order to ensure the longevity of the boat.

2. Aluminum

Aluminum canoes cover a great range of design and quality. The top aluminum canoes are built by Grumman and are used by many tripping camps because of their rugged durability. We tripped with a 17-footer for several years and found it pleasant for lake travel and willing to take lots of abuse. Some people object to these boats because they find them noisy, but once you've acquainted sufficient skill so that you don't bang the boat noisily with each stroke, I don't find the noise of the boat moving through the water all that unpleasant. Their weight is reasonable: 75 pounds for a 17-foot boat.

Once we became involved in whitewater canoeing, however, we noticed that the material does tend to stick to rocks and get hung up on them in places where fiberglass or ABS boats could just slide right over. A coat of butcher's wax helped to an extent, but we eventually replaced the canoe with one we felt better suited us. Another disadvantage the aluminum boat has for whitewater use is that, although the boat is rugged, repair jobs are rather complicated and require riveting on patches of metal. Also, should the boat get hung up on a rock, the aluminum canoe has a tendency to wrap itself around the rock.

3. Fiberglass

Our second boat was constructed of fiberglass, and was a satisfactory and enjoyable boat to use until its premature demise on a rock in a Class III rapid. The material allowed the boat to slide easily over the same rocks that plagued the aluminum canoe and was easy to patch with glass cloth and polyester resin in case of a mishap.

In fact, I think that one of the biggest advantages of fiberglass as a canoe material is that it is easier to repair than any other material.

The quality of fiberglass boats that are on the market varies to an amazing extent, and ranges from some of the finest racing, whitewater and touring boats made to some real tubs! Fiberglass can be shaped into boats of finer lines than can be made with the other materials. So many of the better designs are extremely fast. However, some of the fiberglass canoes on the market are not at all superior in design and can be extremely heavy and awkward.

4. Kevlar

This material is a relative of fiberglass, but since it has different features, I mention it separately here. Kevlar is a new material which takes the best features of fiberglass—slickness and whitewater and flatwater racing, easy and satisfactory reparability—and adds a lot of strength and durability. Many of the manufacturers of fiberglass boats now produce many models in both fiberglass and Kevlar; so that the whitewater enthusiast can buy his choice of canoe in this more sturdy version. The Kevlar canoe is also the most lightweight of canoe material, so it has significant advantages for the canoe camper who is planning a trip that includes portages or carries, or to the racer.

5. ABS

This material was new to the canoe world several seasons back and is now extremely popular, at least in the Northeast where I canoe and where I see more and more ABS canoes each year. Our fleet now consists of two boats made out of this material.

ABS actually consists of a sandwich in which two layers of plastic act as the bread, while a core of foam acts as the peanut butter. The result is an extremely tough material. I've seen these boats wrapped right around rocks but spring right back into shape when released from the obstacle. Our boat bounded off rocks for about a half mile down the Ammonoosuc River after dumping its passenger once last year. The damage it received was so minor we were able to continue the rest of the day with no repair work done at all. After returning home, we patched up the wounded gunwale easily and with little expense.

This material is not without its disadvantages, however. Since it dents rather than breaks, the hull can acquire a rather rippled effect which would detract from its speed and performance in racing. Manufacturers suggest using a warm iron to remove these dents, but the process is not as easy as they make it sound. We even ended up removing some paint. Since we're not involved in racing, we're not as fussy about the aspect as some people, but we've found that leaving the boat out in the sun will smooth out many of the dents to our satisfaction.

While bumping rocks is easily withstood with ABS boats, abrasive situations can lead to minor damage in the outer surface. For example, some friends of ours left their canoe tied at a shore of an isalnd where the bottom was covered with small pebbly rocks. The action of the wind moving the canoe back and forth across these rocks caused part of the outer vinyl layer to rub off. This would not have happened to an aluminum or fiberglass canoe in a similar situation.

The Old Town Canoe Company's "Carleton" canoe.

The structure of a canoe is just as important as the material it is made from. There are many different designs for the many different uses for your canoe. Longer canoes, 18 feet and longer, can hold more gear and people, and generally move faster through the water than canoes of smaller size and similar design. But the added weight may make portaging a difficult task. Canoes of shorter length can suffice for a small family with light, compact camping gear, and their smaller size and weight can make them more manageable when carried.

If you are at all interested in racing, you will want to keep in mind that, not only does the length of the boat affect its speed, so does the width. A narrow boat with a definite point at the bow moves much faster than a wide boat with a blunt end. And a canoe with a V-shape to its hull will be speedier than a flat-bottomed canoe. If you are nervous about the boat's stability, however, or if you intend to use the canoe for fishing, the wider, flatter-bottomed style will be better suited for you. Our canoes have fairly flat bottoms to allow my husband to stand and cast out his fishing line. If we were interested in racing, however, we would certainly make a poor showing in our not-exactly-streamlined canoe!

Wood-canvas and aluminum canoes, and some fiberglass canoes, have an added structure called a keel which runs lengthwise along the center bottom of the boat. The main function of the keel is to help the canoeist maintain a straight course in such conditions as a wind-blown lake. This can be easily accomplished without a keel, and if you intend to do any travelling on shallow rocky streams, a keel can make the boat hang up in places where a keel-less canoe could pass through. In the case of the wood and canvas canoe, the keel also helps to protect the bottom from rocks and such. Aluminum canoes, by the way, are available with a standard keel, which protrudes about an inch and a half, or with a "shoe keel", which is nearly flat. If you will be restricting your travel to lakes and big rivers you could choose the standard keel; if you think you might use the boat in shallow rivers or in whitewater, try the "shoe keel".

Some canoes have thick strips of flotation material along the exterior side of the boat. I don't really feel these are at all necessary, since most modern canoes just aren't that tippy anyway. And, since you may find yourselves quite often in a position where you are passing through a set of rocks or logs where the boat will just barely fit, that added stuff on the sides could make the difference, forcing you to have to fit the canoe over or around the obstacles you would otherwise float between.

A good way to start your canoe search is by assembling literature from many of the different companies producing all of these different types of canoes, and weighing the merits of each against the uses you intend for your canoe. That way, you'll learn a lot about canoes and you'll be able to make a wise choice. You may also want to keep in mind that the interests of your family might change, especially the interests of your children as they become older. You may want to consider a canoe that you feel is versatile and can be used for many purposes on the different kinds of water in your area. Or, you may prefer to choose a specialized canoe which best suits only those uses you know the boat will receive. It's all up to you.

If you want to try camping with a canoe but either can't afford to buy one or aren't ready to buy one yet, most of the well-known canoe regions in the United States and Canada have nearby outfitters who rent canoes and all the other equipment necessary for a canoe camping trip. Some will even plan a trip and pack your food for you. These outfitters advertise in wilderness camping and canoeing publications, or they may be found by inquiring at state agencies and local chambers of commerce.

The gear you bring when canoe camping need not be as extremely light as you would need if you were backpacking. A 16 to 18 foot canoe will carry up to 650 to 775 pounds maximum weight. But your equipment must be compact enough to fit into your craft. If you experiment beforehand and try out different packing methods, you can find out just how much you can bring and how you can best fit your gear and your family into the boat most comfortably. It is also a good idea to try out your fully loaded canoe in the water. You'll find it handles much differently than when it is unloaded. Be sure to always maintain at least a six to eight-inch freeboard for safety. Freeboard is the distance from the surface of the water to the gunwale at the center of the canoe.

With sensible planning and with experimentation, this could be no problem. My husband and I, our two children, all our gear and our sixty-odd pound springer spaniel travel together in our 16-foot Old Town Chipewyan and maintain about a 10 inch freeboard. We may have our problems, but none of them is related to load capacity!

In any case, I think it is a good idea to acquaint your selves with your equipment before you start your trip. Acquire a basic knowledge of the techniques and strokes and practice paddling together to develop a rhythm. Build the muscles you will need on a canoe trip. It's also a good idea to practice ways of lifting the canoe and carrying it. Bring your children on short rides to accustom them to being in a boat and to experiment with comfortable seating arrangements. This may be a full duffel bag turned sideways for a couple of toddlers, a foam pad propped at an angle for an infant.

Life preservers are necessary for both children and adults and are required by law in most states. Don't feel that you are immune to the law because you are out in the wilds. Rangers have been known to fly in and land on lakes in airplanes in order to enforce this rule! You can buy life preservers small enough for

even the tiniest baby. My younger daughter weighed less than ten pounds when we brought her on her first trip, and yet we were able to find one satisfactory for her tiny size. The reason small children must wear them at all times in the canoe is obvious, and I have even required mine to wear them on land in some locations. Some people require their kids to wear them whenever they are even near the water, but I don't feel this is necessary if they are receiving proper supervision. I usually wear one in the canoe myself so that, in case of an upset, I could devote all my attention to the children and would not have to worry about keeping myself afloat at the same time.

Parties of more than one boat greatly increase the safety of any trip. Most sources recommend a minimum of three crafts, but I think two is sufficient, especially if both crews are reasonably responsible and skilled. Having more than one boat in a party is comforting for several reasons—among them the ease of rescue in case of capsizing and the ability to get back to civilization easily even if one boat should become badly damaged for some reason. If a boat capsizes, do not panic. It can be lifted over the other canoe in a procedure called canoe-over-canoe rescue. The water can be easily drained, and your family can climb back in the uprighted boat.

In general, a lake trip with young children is safer than a river trip. Of course, I am assuming that you will take wise precautions in either case. Rescue is simpler without a moving current. This is not to say that a lake is always a safe place for your youngsters, or even for you. High winds can blow up a lake so that its waves are treacherous. In such cases, don't venture out on it. You can always wait until the wind dies down, almost always in the evening and early morning unless a major storm is brewing. If the weather starts to look bad, head for shore.

By staying close to shore and making use of sheltered coves, you may be able to avoid the high waves of the open parts of the lake. Bring along some extra food in case you are forced to wait out a wind. On lake trips, my family generally travels for a few hours in the early morning hours to our new destination. Almost always, by the time the wind picks up, we're already at our new campsite.

If you prefer a river trip, plan to carry around any section of river which you find questionable. If there are rapids, don't over-estimate one's proficiency if there are children in the boat. If you have any questions about your ability to run a certain section of water, carry around it. Or, at least carry or walk the children around it. Sometimes one of us will walk around with the young-sters while the other runs the rapid alone in the boat. What you decide to do is relative to your experience, but should always be approached conservatively and with caution when you are far away from civilization and with children.

Lashing all equipment into the canoe helps to minimize prob-lems should you capsize the canoe. If the boat tips, you don't want your provisions and equipment to sink into the lake or be carried away by the river current. A rope wrapped around the center thwart and laced through each piece of equipment will insure against this.

To avoid upsets (and they happen very rarely, so please don't be alarmed) the best precaution you can take is to stress to your children the importance of sitting still in the canoe. If you have a dog along, he may be more of a problem. Many times our stability has been threatened when Freckles has decided to jump to the other side of the boat to inspect a group of ducks more closely! If children lean over the side, as ours have been prone to do when they were smaller, they are more apt to fall in than tip the boat. This is still a problem, especially if the water or the weather is cold. But again let me stress that these events are extremely rare and usually avoidable. When they do happen, they are usually inconvenient more than frightening. The only mishap we've ever had as a family was when our obstinate one-year-old insisted on standing and leaning over to look into the water when we were fishing off shore from our campsite one evening. She ended up getting a very close—and wet—look! But, while we thought the experience might at least teach her a lesson the hard way, she didn't seem to mind it in the least, and maybe even enjoyed the diversion! Since she was wearing an approved life vest, it flipped her right-side-up immediately, and she was retrieved from the water within seconds.

Canoe loaded for a one week trip.

My husband and I used to discount practically any trip which required long portages. We felt that the hassle of carrying all the gear, the boat, and possibly the kids was more trouble than it could be worth to get to the other side of the trail. But, lately, we've started to include portages in our itinerary. We've discovered that, not only do we not mind them, we actually enjoy them. So do our girls. The break in the routine of paddling is refreshing, and we get a chance to stretch our legs and to see some features of the land we would otherwise miss. We found that we could easily complete a portage with the children making one trip across the trail, and each of us adults making two. And this was a two-week trip; so we had a full load of gear and food. The children each carried their own clothing on their backs. My husband carried the canoe and a small day pack on his first trip and a duffel rigged with a tump-line on the second. I walked with the children on my first trip, carrying on my back a fairly light pack filled with clothing, with sleeping bags tied on top and bottom. My second trip I carried a heavier pack. We made certain that there was always an adult with the children on the portage trail, and at the end while they waited for us to complete carrying the gear across. Since another family was above, this was not difficult to maintain. Each adult would simply wait with the children until the next adult appeared before returning for another load. This way, our portages were not only feasible, they were actually fun! If you intend to portage, it helps if the gear is brought along in easily carried containers such as packs. It also helps to plan to travel as light as possible.

If your children enjoy the trip, you're more likely to have a good time. Pace your trip with their interests in mind. If your journey is too long each day, toddlers will become fidgety and, if your children are older, you may have a full-fledged mutiny on your hands! On the other hand, a baby probably won't mind a bit and will probably allow you to travel just as long as you like. I

found the gentle rocking motion of the boat moving through the water generally put my babies right to sleep. If you devise a comfortable place for an infant to ride with her face shaded from the sun, conditions are even better for sleeping. This may involve a bit of trial and error with different means of padding, considering the awkward bouyancy of materials characteristic of most children's life jackets, but comfortable accommodations can be arranged.

The basic techniques of paddling a canoe can be learned easily and quickly by consulting a book such as the Red Cross canoeing manual, and practicing them out on a flat piece of water. If you will be paddling a canoe tandem, it will probably be easiest to manage if the stronger person paddles in back at the stern. On flat water, the stern will be doing most of the steering, and will be able to function best if he masters the J-stroke, the draw and the pry, as well as developing an effective forward paddling technique.

As well as a good forward paddling form, the bowman needs to know some steering strokes. Quick bow maneuverability is important in a current—especially to avoid rocks and other obstacles the stern paddler may not see. As you progress to whitewater canoeing, the bow will have even more work to do and sharing the maneuvering duties about equally with the stern. Helmets should be required for tricky rapids.

If you will be paddling with one person per canoe, it is easiest to manage the boat from near the center, rather than from either of the canoe seats. The solo paddler must know the steering strokes, obviously, since he is alone in determining where the boat will go.

While we are on the subject of position in the boat, the question of to kneel or not to kneel comes up. While all mass produced family canoes that I know of come equipped with seats, much of the traditional canoe lore has stressed the importance of kneeling in a canoe. On smooth, flat water, I think it is mainly a question of personal preference, and doesn't make a heck of a lot of difference. Some people are more comfortable paddling from a sitting position, some from a kneeling position. Myself, I like to alternate on a long trip. I paddle from a kneeling position for a period of time, but if I feel my legs starting to get stiff or cramped up from maintaining that position, I sit for a while. On choppy water, such as a lake stirred up by a high wind, the stability of the canoe is increased if the paddlers stay in a kneeling position. With the knees braced against the sides of the canoe, one has a firmer position from which to lean over the side of the boat and make a bold steering stroke. Kneeling is also a far more effective position for canoeing in rapids. We make it a rule to kneel even in easy rapids.

If you watch a group of canoeists, you will notice that, even if they have a comparable amount of skill and experience, their forward paddling movements will be quite varied. I think developing an effective forward paddling stroke is mainly a question of finding the best and most comfortable way to execute a stroke which will work well towards propelling the boat through the water. Some people are most comfortable with their lower hand close to the hand at the top of the paddle. Others find they function better with their hands spread wider apart, with their second hand close to the beginning of the blade of the paddle. Some people prefer to lean forward with each stroke, using the upper part of the body to help pull the paddle through the water. Others prefer to let their arms and shoulders do the job. Your individual strengths and weaknesses, and the dictation of your own comfort will determine what kind of forward paddling stroke you develop. Work on a stroke that will pull the paddle through the water for a long enough distance and with a strong enough force behind it to move the boat effectively.

The draw stroke is the simplest of the steering strokes. To complete this stroke the paddler reaches out over the side of the canoe on which he normally paddles, puts the paddle into the water so that the blade is parallel to the side of the boat, and pulls it through the water towards him. The stroke is most effective when the paddler reaches far out over the gunwale; so don't be afraid to lean out there—the canoe has enough stability to handle it if you are working from a kneeling position with knees braced. Properly executed, this stroke will move the canoe sideways in the water with little forward motion.

Pulling the canoe in the opposite direction than the one in which one normally paddles can be achieved by the cross-draw, in which one maintains the same hand positions, but crosses the paddle over to the other side of the canoe. Put the paddle into the water with the blade parallel to the side of the canoe and pull the paddle toward the boat. Since this stroke involves crossing to the other side of the canoe, it is frowned upon by many canoeists. They prefer, instead, to use the pry stroke. In this stroke, the paddle is inserted in the water right next to the side of the boat in a vertical position. Then, using the gunwale as a fulcrum, the blade is pushed away from the side of the boat in one strong motion.

The purpose of the J-stroke is to keep the canoe moving forward on a straight course. The solo paddler and the stern paddler of a tandem boat use this stroke or a variation of it as often as needed, in many cases almost continually. This stroke begins as a regular forward paddling stroke but, about half way through, the paddler starts to turn the blade sideways very gradually by rotating the wrists, and ends the stroke by pushing it away from the canoe to execute a "j" or hook. When first learning this stroke, one may use the gunwale of the canoe as a fulcrum to push off of; but this should not be necessary after sufficient practice. Since this can be a rather difficult stroke to master, and since it can be a tiring stroke, you may want to investigate one of its many variations, or you may want to develop one of your own that will effectively keep the canoe on a straight course.

Once you've learned the strokes, you're ready for canoe camping, one of the most enjoyable and relaxing ways to spend a vacation that I know. The joys of canoe camping really can't be expressed. You have to try it to believe just how much fun it can be. When hearing about our adventures canoe-camping with our young daughters, some of my friends say "You call THAT a vacation?!" I agree with them. There are many times, after a full day of paddling, portaging, fishing, swimming, and playing, that I sit by a campfire with my family and listen to the loons calling to each other across the dark water. We must find a much more beautiful name for it.

8. FAMILY BICYCLING

Many areas of the United States, both developed and rural, are ideal for exploring by bicycle. And, if you want to become an international traveller, many other countries are even better suited for this kind of travel. Since bicycling is such a common means of transportation in Europe, the accommodations for bicyclists there are especially inviting. Bicycling, involves a direct relationship with the environment. By this I mean that the weather means more than just having to turn on the windshield wipers and that the scenery isn't separated from you by a piece of glass. Also, you move under your own power and are dependent upon your own energies.

Typically, bicycle camping would involve going a certain distance each day and setting up camp, carrying your own lightweight gear with you on your bicycle in handlebar packs and panniers. I have seen people carry large packs on their backs while bicycling, but to me this is too uncomfortable to be practical, too unstable to be safe. By carefully reducing your gear to the minimum and reprovising along the way where it is possible, and by investing in some of the carefully designed bicycle pack equipment, I think carrying anything more than a small day pack on your back is probably highly unnecessary.

In order to effectively participate on a trip of this nature, on his own bike, a child probably would have to be at least eight years

The place to learn how to ride a bike is in a safe area around your neighborhood. Supervision and support help when you are starting out.

Just as when you were learning to drive a car, learning bicycling "rules of the road" and safety tips is essential.

old. Eye and motor coordination is not the only factor affecting this judgement. A fairly long attention span is necessary in order for a child to keep his mind on what he is doing long enough to bicycle safely for a long period of time, or even to want to bicycle for a long period of time. Physical development is also important.

If you feel your child is ready for this type of experience, observe his bicycling habits closely and make sure he is progressing towards being a good and careful bicyclist. A few family day trips in which you cover a distance comparable to that which you intend to cover daily on your trip would be a good testing and training ground for children and adults alike, and would give you an excellent chance to observe your family's performance beforehand. This will also help you in planning the trip. You may find that your expectations were unrealistic, and that you will want to reduce the projected distance you had planned for a day's trip. Or, your family may surprise you with its endurance, and you may find your estimates too conservative. In any case, these day trips should be enjoyable anyway.

But even if you are satisfied that your child's riding skill and endurance are suitable for a bicycle trip, he or she may not have the strength and coordination necessary to carry much of the camping gear. A set of loaded panniers affects not only the bicycle's weight, but its handling and maneuverability. If you are expecting your children to carry gear along on the trip, by all means have them practice before-hand with loaded carriers. Take them to an empty parking lot and make a game of trying to ride along one of the long painted lines. If the added weight creates too much wobbling, they are not ready to ride on roads, and are apt to be uncomfortable even on back roads without traffic.

This is an excellent time to make sure your kids are thoroughly familiar with hand signals, safety precautions, and rules of the road in your area and state. This is even more important when they are loaded up with trip gear and can be more easily distracted. It would not be a bad idea to put them through an actual test to get a parental "license" before they can go out on public roads.

What do you do if your children are not mature enough to carry gear, or even to ride their own bicycles on a trip? If the child is young and small enough, you can transport him on your own bike. You may reduce your gear to a bare minimum by relying on hostels for overnight accommodations. Another feasible way to travel is to use one of the bicycle trailers now on the market. These are contraptions which look something like a rick-shaw and attach to the rear of an adult-size bicycle. They have two large wheels and are used most commonly to transport gear. The trailer can be used to pull camping gear, allowing the child to ride in a child-carrier seat on the other parent's bike. In this way, the problem of transporting both child and gear can be solved.

I must admit that I was doubtful about the manufacturer's claim that an average woman could easily pull two four-year-olds in this apparatus until we purchased one two years ago. I found it relatively easy to pull both children (totalling about 100 lbs.) even up some fairly steep hills. The two-wheeled trailer makes a bicycle remarkably stable, enabling you to virtually inch up a steep grade. Our bike trailer transformed my bicycle into a sort of second car for us, freeing me to do errands around town with the children, at least during the snow-free months of the year.

Best of all, the trailer gave us the flexibility to go camping on our bicycles. Our two children—just 1 year apart in age—took turns alternating between a 20 inch bicycle and a kiddy seat on the back of my bike. All of our camping gear was pulled in the trailer behind my husband. Even on day trips the trailer was helpful, especially when the girls had more or less outgrown the kiddy seat but neither had the stamina to last on a day-long ride. By alternating between the trailer and the bicycle, each was able to enjoy a long tour.

While the trailer can be quite expensive—as much as $200 complete with passenger seat—it can be a sensible investment for a family that enjoys biking. And, unlike the kiddy seat which outlives its usefulness and is destined for some future yard sale, the trailer is permanently useful. Once the children are on their

own wheels, it can be used for camping gear, groceries, library books etc., until you're ready to start transporting grandchildren in it!

There are many types of bicycle child carriers or "kiddy seats" available on the market. Some have questionable looking seat belts and side supports. I consider a good bicycle seat for a child to be one which supports the child well in back and on each side, has a strong safety belt system and a foot guard to keep the child's feet from the spokes of the rear wheel. I especially like the molded plastic "bucket seat" type. It looks comfortable, has all of the features I've mentioned and, since it offers such good back and side support, I found my daughter could use it at a very early age, younger than her sister was first able to use one of the more conventional child seats.

Let's assume that you cannot afford to buy a bike trailer, and the part of the country your family wants to explore by bicycle is one which does not contain a good number of hostels. Still determined to go? My husband has devised an excellent plan which we never did get to try. The problem was finding another interested couple before our older daughter reached that awkward stage when she was too heavy to ride on our bikes, too young to ride her own for a long distance. The plan, you see, involves more than one family. The method uses a car to transport gear. Each day, one adult and one child "sit out." Instead of bicycling, they ride in the transport car and move the gear to the bicyclists' destination, the next campsite. By taking turns, each adult can bike three days out of four. Or, if you split each day into halves and switch drivers at a lunch spot, everyone could bicycle at least part of each day. This is a reasonable compromise for the years when your children are small. Another sensible alternative is to stay at hostels and bring only the minimum amount of gear needed in that situation.

I think it's advisable for all family members to get used to riding with extra weight before you begin your trip. Carrying extra weight affects the bike's stability, and may take getting used to. It also helps to get used to packing your gear so that it is comfortable and doesn't severely hamper you. You may get a better idea of just how much weight it's feasible for you to carry on your bicycle.

If you have a little passenger on the back of your bike, it's important to watch your speed on hills and rough terrain, not only for the child's safety, but for her comfort and enjoyment as well. Where possible, my husband and I try to keep an eye on the child on the other's bike as well as our own passenger. Sometimes a problem is first apparent to the other adult, and can be corrected more readily if both are watching out.

A bicycling helmet is an important piece of equipment. These are now available in sizes for youngsters as well as adults. Another useful piece of safety equipment is a small rear-view mirror. These mirrors are available in two styles: one clips on to a standard biker's helmet; the other attaches to a pair of glasses or sunglasses. Their purpose is to allow a bicyclist to view the road behind without turning her head, an action which tends to veer the bike slightly to the side and can lead to loss of control. A loud air horn is also useful, both in traffic and in discouraging dog attacks.

Some people carry an eye-irritating aerosol spray or a squirt-gun filled with ammonia and water to ward off unfriendly dogs. I have found neither to be of great use. I stopped bringing squirt guns after smashing at least a half dozen by dropping them on the pavement. And, after using a whole can of aerosol on an unfriendly sheep dog-type without ever getting through to his eyes, I stopped buying that! In addition, having such products along means just one more item to try to keep out of the kids' reach.

Dogs, however, can be a big problem. On the lightly travelled country roads most inviting for bike travel, they are probably **the** biggest problem. Even a friendly dog can make trouble for you. My two-year-old and I were once overturned by a congenial golden retriever who tagged along beside us for a ways, then decided to cross the street, walking right into the wheel of my bicycle.

The most recommended way to deal with an unfriendly dog is not to try to out-speed him, but to dismount and walk the bicycle. This way, the dog at least is able to view you as human, rather than as some unidentified moving object. With careful maneuvering, you can usually keep your bicycle between you

This group is ready for a day trip. Note the helmets and handlebar bags which contain tools for repairs besides maps, snacks, and a camera.

and all but the most persistent dog, for protection. Quite often, a strong blast of your air horn will confuse the animal into keeping his distance.

In choosing a bicycle for an older child, it's important not to bite off more than she can chew. It's wisest not to buy a bicycle too big for a child to "grow into." Trying to manage a bicycle that is too large or too advanced can be not only discouraging, but downright unsafe. From her first two-wheeler, probably a 20 inch wheel model with coaster brakes, a child may advance to a small 3-speed with a simplified shifting system which allows the changing of gears while coasting. Finally, your child can graduate to a full-size, ten-speed bicycle. While a three-speed may be sufficient for the whole family on easy trips on flat terrain, a good lightweight 10-speed bicycle is recommended for serious touring.

Even on day trips, it's wise to carry a first aid kit, a tool kit, spare tire tubes, and a manual for repairs. Bike shops sell special kits containing the tools needed for bicycle repairs, or you may put together your own combination of screw drivers and pliers. A five-way combination tool can be a compact way to bring the tools you may find you need. The practice of bringing along a tool kit has saved us from many an unpleasant experience. Even if there is no real emergency, a minor derailleur adjustment or the correction of an annoying rub or squeak can make your ride so much more enjoyable.

Hats, sun screen and rain gear are also good to carry on your bike. They won't do you much good in your transport car at the other end of the day's ride.

By bringing our children along on our bicycles, we are encouraging them to seek out a wholesome way of life. I look forward to the day when we can take a long bicycle trip together with our kids on their own bikes. Maybe if enough of us get our children used to travelling by people-power, we'll lick the pollution problems yet! Not to mention the fuel shortage....

9. STAYING HEALTHY

To stay healthy on your trip, make sure you're healthy before you start. If you are used to moderate exercise, and exercise regularly, and if you've had a physical examination within the past year and have received a clean bill of health or have any health problem that may have been discovered well under control, you are probably well prepared for the trip. If, however, you have been physically inactive, or have not had a recent examination, or if you are at all suspicious about a possible health problem, a bit of background work is required before you're going to have a safe and enjoyable trip.

A physical examination can make your trip more pleasant by giving you some peace of mind, especially if you are nervous about any physical condition you have or think you might have. Most young children are examined regularly and receive needed inoculations such as tetanus at the prescribed intervals. Many adults (and I confess to being guilty of this many times myself) often approach their own medical care in a more casual way. I think it's wise to update your medical care before you undertake a rigorous extended outdoor activity, especially if you have let yourself become sedentary. Most doctors advise people to have a physical examination before beginning any new exercise program, and if you are just starting out skiing, bicycling, or carrying a pack on your back or a canoe on your shoulders, you are undertaking a new form of exercise.

119

If you are unused to regular exercise, your trip can be more pleasurable if you begin some type of exercise routine to build your body up before you start out on your trip. Hiking, skiing, canoeing or bicycling for gradually longer intervals is very valuable, but so is a program of general conditioning exercises. Many YMCAs and other health clubs often offer such programs, as do public adult education centers in many towns and cities. If none of these is available or convenient for you, your local library or bookstore has books that can help you develop your own exercise program at home.

Children, even though most of them get plenty of exercise when they're playing, also benefit from an exercise program. It need not, and should not, be rigidly structured, but can be turned into a fun time for you and your children. Such games as wheelbarrow races and duck-waddling parades help to strengthen muscles your child may not often use in his play, and can be a lot of fun for everyone. Last winter my children attended a "swim and gym" course at our nearby YMCA where they were introduced to an exercise program and received swimming training as well—both beneficial to the child who spends much of the summer canoe-camping. If your child is attending school, you may want to investigate the physical education program there and find exercises to supplement the program if you feel it is lacking in any area.

To maintain peak fitness on your trip, many people advise bringing along a multiple vitamin supplement. While this is not essential, it can be reassuring, especially if you are at all concerned about the nutritional balance of the foods you have brought along, or if your children are very fussy eaters who may not be depended upon to eat the variety of foods provided.

I think it's also an excellent idea for at least one member of the family, and hopefully more than one, to enroll in a course in first aid. Even if you never go camping, this kind of knowledge is valuable in so many instances, both at home and away. And just knowing that you are prepared for emergencies can make you much more confident and secure. These courses are offered at colleges, health clubs, adult education centers, and hospitals. Police and fire departments often sponsor such courses for the citizens of their town. No matter where you live in this nation, you should be able to find such a course offered within a reasonable distance from your home. The Red Cross can be consulted for information about the availability of these courses. As well as the general first aid course (which is often offered on two levels, First Aid and Advanced First Aid), many hospitals, fire and police departments and other public service agencies often sponsor courses in cardio-pulmonary rescue.

All in all, I think it is at least a good idea to know the basics of first aid treatment, including a mastery of the techniques of artificial respiration and cardio-pulmonary resuscitation. You won't feel confident learning these from a book. Instructors are equipped with learning devices constructed to teach these methods and test your mastery of the skills. If you have mastered those skills to such an extent that you can pass these tests, your confidence that you can put your knowledge to work will be increased.

The first aid kit itself should be kept in a waterproof container and checked and restocked if necessary before each trip. A first aid manual should always be included and can be a good source to consult for a list of what to include in your kit. Different authors of manuals prescribe a wide range of supplies, from the rather basic list offered by the *Reader's Digest Guide to First Aid* to Dr. Russel Kodet's *Being Your Own Wilderness Doctor*. Many of the more advanced books include the use of prescription drugs, something you may not want to get involved in, or may be unable to get involved in if you can't find a doctor who is willing to help you procure these drugs. The following is a basic list of what I consider important to bring, but this is largely a personal matter, and your own confidence in handling medicine and the special health problems you or members of your family might have may require that you add other items to the list that follows:

Sterile gauze pads, 4" × 4"
Roll of 2" gauze bandage
Roll of adhesive tape
Band-Aids
Butterfly bandages (These are used for holding closed large
    wounds. Some authors recommend bringing sutures.)

Triangular bandage
Antiseptic cream or ointment
Calamine or similar lotion (for poison ivy, sunburn, etc.)
Ammonia inhalants
Scissors (You may want the folding kind.)
Tweezers
Needle (The needle in your mending kit can double.)
Matches
Oral thermometer
Rectal thermometer
Aspirin (Include baby aspirin if you have small children, or
    familiarize yourself with the proportion of adult aspirin
    which is appropriate for your child. You may want to tape
    this information on the side of the kit.)
Syrup of ipecac (to induce vomiting)
Mineral Oil (also in case of poisoning)
First aid manual

The syrup of ipecac and the mineral oil are especially important for the family which includes young children. It is extremely important that you use the appropriate remedy for the
particular poison ingested. Inducing vomiting can cause further
and more serious complications in some cases than the original
swallowing of the poison. If the poison is a volatile substance,
such as kerosene or gasoline, the mineral oil, not the ipecac
syrup, is what to use. This is also true in the case of a strong acid
or an alkali substance such as drain opener, but it is unlikely that
your child would find these on a camping trip.

Depending upon the personal health conditions of members
of your family, you may feel the need to add to this kit. For
example, if any member of your family is known to be extremely
sensitive to insect bites, your physician may supply you with a
prescription of Cortisone or with a special kit containing adrenal-
ine and other necessary items for use in the event of being stung
while away from civilization. You may simply want to include some
pills to combat a pollen allergy some member of your family might
have. Or, for a still less dramatic example, you may want to bring
along a nasal aspirator for a baby or toddler prone to congestion.

If you are in snake country, a snake bit kit should be included in your gear. There are several different kinds, all utilizing suction to draw out the venom from the wound, and they are sold by most wilderness supply houses. There is some debate about the safety of the use of the kits themselves. If you are within a short distance from civilization, prompt evacuation may be the best course.

In case you must evacuate for any emergency reason, I think it is a good idea to know, before you leave the roads, just where the nearest hospital, forest ranger, police or rescue department is located. That way, if an emergency strikes, you won't have to waste valuable time trying to find your way to someone who can help you. If you are venturing so far from the beaten path that you can't evacuate readily in case of emergency, you can purchase a signal device from your outfitter or wilderness camping store to take along on your trip. Most areas have fire watch-towers and some are regularly patrolled by plane as well. Chances are good that, properly equipped, you may be able to make your situation known and get help in evacuating an injured party. These distress signal devices consist of a flare mounted on a firing pin so they can be fired high into the air where they burn with a colored smoke that is visible day or night. Failing that, one could build a smoky fire with green branches thrown on.

If you are backpacking, or if you are canoeing on a trip which includes long portages, you will probably want to include moleskin in your first aid kit. Blisters are probably the most painful problem a hiker is likely to have, and can usually be prevented. If your boots fit properly, and if you change socks regularly (at least once or twice daily) and use the two-sock method, you can probably avoid them altogether. Socks can be washed out and hung to dry on the pack while hiking, so the quantity of socks need not be a problem. If an area starts to become raised and sensitive, a layer of moleskin can often prevent it from developing into a full-fledged blister. If a blister does develop, it is probably best treated by lancing it with a sterilized needle, applying a small amount of your antiseptic cream or ointment, and then covering it first with a bandaid and then with a layer of moleskin. When the day's hiking is over, you may want to expose the area to the sun and air to help it heal.

On most trips you will probably never even open your first aid kit, except for a possible band-aid here and there for skinned knees and elbows. In all our years of wilderness camping, five of them with the children, we've never had any serious emergency. But of course it's important to always be prepared for anything that might happen, and that's what the first aid kit and the knowledge to use it are all about.

Undoubtedly one of the best ways to stay healthy on your trip is to stay clear of unnecessarily dangerous situations. A prime example of this is early spring canoeing. There are two factors which make canoeing in the early spring highly dangerous. One (and this is true at other times of year after extremely heavy rains) is flooding. An extremely high water level can greatly affect the safety of canoeing on a normally reasonable river. My husband and I almost got ourselves into a lot of trouble this way when we were first starting out as canoeists. Water conditions were so high one day that the backwater above a dam was literally non-existent—a full current was charging right over the falls. Luckily we spotted power lines over the river ahead of us and were alerted in time to pull out well before rounding the bend above the dam. The second danger to springtime canoeing is water temperature. A dunking in near-freezing water is no joke. It is not merely a matter of discomfort but is downright dangerous! Many people die each year because of immersion in the icy water of early spring. The water is debilitating and paralyzing, making it difficult not only to swim, but even to breathe. Whitewater enthusiasts, who find that many of their favorite streams can be run only when they are cold, protect themselves by wearing divers' wet suits. Even these do not protect indefinitely, and most experienced canoeists will get out of the cold water at the very earliest opportunity.

So as you can see, this not the place for family outings. If you are really anxious to get in your canoe, it's a warm day, and you have brought an extra set of clothing for each person in the boat, it's probably okay on a flat piece of water you are well familiar with. Under these conditions, it is mandatory that **everyone** wear lifejackets. And, when dressing for the outing, remember the merits, discussed earlier, of wool and *Polar Guard*®. Make sure the extra set of clothing is in a waterproof bag and is secured so that it won't end up washing downstream in case of an upset. Generally speaking, I really can't recommend canoeing on icy waters as a family if you have very young children.

Another culprit related to cold temperatures that affects the body is frostbite. Frostbite first makes itself evident by causing a patch of skin to turn white or pale yellowish. This is not easily noticed by the affected individual himself, but can be noted by a comparison. Make it a policy between members of the party to keep an eye on each other and watch for signs of frostbite on cold and windy days. The person skiing alone can try to keep on the alert for the tingling sensation which usually accompanies the change in color of the skin. Most sources recommend immersion of the affected area in tepid water (about 102°) as a remedy, but if you are out for a day's ski, you may warm a hand by placing it under an armpit. Avoiding extremely cold days for a family ski trip is a good idea. In the future, you want your children to look forward to another day of skiing, not dread it. Of course one must be especially careful about cold windy days and extremely low temperatures if a skier is carrying a baby on his back. Since the child doesn't get the exercise you do, he is even more susceptible to the extremes in temperature.

The most extreme cold weather disaster is hypothermia. This is basically the lowering of the body temperature to the point of death. Hypothermia is brought on by exposure to extreme cold, either from weather or water (mentioned earlier). Check your kids constantly (and yourself for drowsiness) in bitter cold situations, also after extreme temperature drops (especially after a freezing rain). It is imperative to raise the body temperature **FAST** through hot liquids, dry blankets, and warmth (fire). Hopefully you will never find yourself or your kids in this predicament.

Just as extremely cold temperatures can be dangerous, so can extreme heat. If a person who has been exerting himself in extreme heat becomes pale and complains of weakness or dizziness, heat exhaustion should be suspected. Other symptoms are profuse sweating or clamminess. The treatment is rest in a cooler location. Heat stroke is a much more serious problem where the body temperature rises dangerously, and death can occur. The symptoms are different from heat exhaustion, since the skin appears hot and dry, and vomiting and nausea are often present. Treatment is to lower the body temperature by bathing in cool water, the same way one lowers the temperature of a child with a high fever. Luckily, heat stroke is not often a problem except in extremely hot climates, and then it usually affects mostly those who are in poor physical condition. Nevertheless it can happen to anyone; so you should be aware of it.

The least sophisticated but most common health problem campers usually encounter on a trip is known by various names such as the "Green Apple Two-Step" or "Montezuma's Revenge." Or, simply diarrhea. While many factors may cause this problem, the fitness of the water supply and the diligence of the dishwasher are usually the culprits. Any drinking water which comes from a questionable source can be treated with halazone or iodine tablets to insure its safeness. And careful washing of the dishes at least once a day with soap and hot water (being sure to rinse them carefully) can eliminate that as a source of the affliction.

All told, I think the best way to stay healthy on a camping trip is to start healthy and choose your location and activities wisely. Try to avoid situations and conditions where problems are most likely to occur, and pace your trip to your family's comfort. Chances are that you will never need your first aid supplies and know-how. But having them handy is your health insurance policy for wilderness travel.

10. A WILDERNESS ADVENTURE

Early Friday morning we left our home not far from Fitchburg, Massachusetts and headed toward the heart of Maine. Our destination was a chain of lakes deep in the heart of the paper companies' forest lands in the northeast part of the state. We had been there before, every year in fact, since we had first discovered it. This was a favorite spot of ours, and we eagerly looked forward to getting there and starting our trip. We were to join up with another family of friends—an old college buddy of my husband, his wife, and his two children (a six-year-old boy and a seven-year-old girl). Our own daughters were one and two.

After about eight hours of driving, the last hour or two over dirt roads, we arrived at the lake where we would begin our trip. Only a few fisherman were present. Some were staying in a pick-up camper at the end of the road, while others were camped down by the campsite where we were headed. No problem. We knew that the campsite area had plenty of spaces cleared out so that we could all stay there and not even be close enough to notice one another. We loaded our gear, our children, our dog, ourselves into the canoe and paddled about a half hour down the lake to set up camp on a point separating two arms of the lake. We were glad it was no farther because the long drive was tiring.

Here I should probably explain a bit about Maine's relationship with the paper companies. The state and the paper manufacturers have a good kind of symbiotic relationship. While the paper companies own most of the forest lands in Maine, they allow campsites to be cut out in designated spots and used by the general public. The state forestry service, in turn, maintains the campsites and patrols the area. But don't think that means you're apt to see little government boats puttering around all the time. In five years of camping in this area, sometimes more than once a year, I've only seen a ranger once.

After setting up camp, we cooked the last meal of fresh food for several days—chicken, potatoes and onions baked over the fire. Our friends arrived shortly after we finished eating. After a little fireside talk, accompanied by toasted marshmallows, we all went to bed in order to get an early start the next morning.

After a quick breakfast, we broke camp, packed up and headed down the lake. On mornings like this, in order to get an early start, my husband and I try to divide the work so that we can finish and leave as soon as possible. He starts breakfast while I help the kids get dressed, pack up the clothes, and start stuffing the sleeping bags. When breakfast is ready, we eat together; then I clean up and pack the food and mess kit while he finishes the sleeping bags and takes down the tent. As a result, the whole process is amazingly fast. What takes the longest is getting the kids to eat their breakfast. Since they are rather poky eaters, they sometimes end up finishing their breakfasts in the canoe.

At the end of the lake, we carried the gear and canoes around an old wooden dam and entered the narrow stream which would take us to the next lake. The trip down the stream was fun—full of little, easy rapids and riffles. There was no danger, since the water was very low. The only challenge was to find the channel where the water was deep enough for the boat to pass. In several spots there was no such channel, and Jack and I had to hop out and wade the boat through until there was a spot where there was enough water to float the boat again. Farther down the stream, we got to a marshier section. A Great Blue Heron flew up in front of us, his long legs sticking out behind him. He looked like a creature from a prehistoric time. The kids were amazed to see the size of his footprints in the mud at the side of the stream. As we entered the lake, another bird flew over us, high overhead, and

I took out the binoculars. We've seen bald eagles in this area, but the glasses proved this one to be an osprey.

As we started paddling up the lake, we congratulated ourselves on the early start we got that morning. The wind was starting to pick up, and we might have had a hard paddle to our campsite if we were an hour or so late. The site we were heading to is one of our favorites, a point sticking out into the lake with a beautiful beach of fine sand going around all three sides, facing the water.

The campsite was even better than we remembered. Since it was a hot, sunny day, we would spend the whole afternoon swimming and lying in the sun, while the children dug in the sand and played at the edge of the water.

After supper, we paddled around a bit, exploring a rocky island not far off shore from our camp. The other family went fishing, and caught some fine white perch.

Next morning my husband and older daughter dressed early and went fishing while my younger daughter and I stayed in the tent late playing guessing games, talking, and snuggling. We had just come out of the tent when the others were back with enough perch and bass to make a nice fish breakfast. We cooked the fish and some dried hash brown potatoes we had brought along, and enjoyed a leisurely breakfast since we were not moving camp that day. Our friends had good luck fishing that morning, too, and after a brief pow-wow, we decided to stay at this spot longer than we had planned.

The following days at the campsite on the lake passed with more swimming and fishing. We hiked up a trail out of camp and found some blueberries which added interest to the next morning's pancakes. Another day, we paddled down to the dam at the end of the lake to take a look at the river which starts there. That river, a fairly wild and remote stream, mostly flat but containing several long and interesting rapids, is a trip we're looking forward to doing another year when the kids are a little bigger. At the dam we met some other campers who told us about a spring on a trail leading up from a point on the shore on the way back to camp. We found it and had a refreshing drink of cold water.

The last day, when it was time to go home, we paddled to the north end of the lake and up a canal which was dug by some incredibly ambitious individual many years before. Last time my husband and I had been there, travelling the canal involved pushing the canoe through crotch-deep mud. We were happy that the water level meant easy going this time. Two pretty, wild ponds and two short stretches of stream brought us to the final lake, where we reluctantly paddled across to the car.

A simple trip marked by a lot of good fun and companionship had drawn to a close. We found ourselves planning a future trip with our friends before we parted company and headed home!

11. THE JOYS OF CAMPING

Just what does draw some of us to the woods, and keeps us going back there, year after year? There are a lot of reasons why different people are turning to the wilderness for their recreation. Some are conscious, while others are known only to our inner selves. For many, I think it is a reaction against the automated world where the social security identification number becomes more important than a person's name; where letters are answered by computer and where individuals feel lost in the lonely crowd.

For others, life in the wilderness, even in small doses, is a chance to relive the simplified existence of the early voyageurs and pioneers. For them, the wilderness has a nostalgic appeal related to a longing to return to a more primitive lifestyle.

Still others find the study of Nature's ecology intriguing. Nature lovers appreciate the opportunity to observe wild animals in their own habitat. My children were much more excited about surprising a group of otters at play in a river pool than they have ever been about looking at animals through bars or glass windows at the zoo. Their curiosity about the otters was matched by the curiosity with which the otters stared at them. They are both Nature's creatures, each interested and respectful of the other.

The serious athlete can find plenty of challenges in the wilderness against which to test his own skills, strengths, and fitness.

And even those of us who aren't so serious or athletic can gain a tremendous satisfaction when we've reached the top of a mountain or the end of a portage trail, or when we've skied down a long hill. For young children, even the simplest task can be a challenge which, when completed, has great rewards. The first thing our daughters told their friends when they returned from one trip early this year was that they had carried all their own clothes on their backs all week! If the friends could have seen the steep rocky sections of some of the trails where those clothes were carried, I'm sure they'd be impressed.

Some find the solitude that can be found in the wilderness reason enough to want to spend time there. Away from the intrusions of civilization—jangling telephones, supermarket lines, chain link fences—life can take on a new perspective.

Some parents enjoy a wilderness vacation because they can allow their children a freer rein than most vacation spots encourage. Playing in the dirt and making a lot of noise won't be offensive to anyone if nobody is around to be offended.

For families whose budgets are limited, the wilderness offers an unlimited number of economy vacations. This year we spent two weeks in an absolutely beautiful part of the Canadian interior. At one stop, the scenery included an impressive 39-foot waterfall, while another day we had a half-mile sandy beach all to ourselves. No resort vacation, which we probably couldn't afford anyway, has features such as these.

Why do I like wilderness camping? One reason is certainly a feeling of closeness to Nature that one can only get by living in its midst. You become alert to slight changes in the weather, to the sound and the sights and the smells that you miss by just taking an occasional short walk through the woods.

I like being in the wilderness because it helps me put my values and priorities back into order. The materialistic wants that I sometimes have are put into a better perspective after I've lived in the woods for a week and realize that food, clothing, a little bit of shelter and some human companionship are all I really need to get by in this world.

Another reason I like to go camping with my family is that it reinforces my faith in us as a family unit. I'm sure all of us have had bad days. You know, those days when the kids are bickering and fighting, and you feel your temper becoming shorter and shorter? You begin to wonder where you're headed. But if we can live together in the woods for a week or longer, having no contact with any other people except maybe a wave to someone in a passing canoe, and still love and enjoy each other, I feel we must be pretty close after all.

I love the wilderness because I feel at home there—a part of a naturally ordered existence. And I like it when my children feel this, too. One evening, when we were fishing, my younger daughter said to me, "Mommy, I want to go home now."

A little taken aback, I said, "But, Honey, we won't be going back home till next week."

"No, *that* home," she said, pointing to the bluff where we were camped. She felt at home in the wilderness.

Even though we enjoy camping with friends, it's important to me to take at least one trip a year alone with my husband and children. There are so few opportunities in these hurried times for the kind of communication that can develop when you are alone with each other and dependent upon each other in the woods. Perhaps there would be less of a generation gap in families where this kind of communication was encouraged to take place. I hope this will be the case as our children become older.

By bringing our daughters camping in the wilderness, I hope we are laying the groundwork for a life lived close to nature. I hope that the girls will maintain the relationship they seem to be developing with the out-of-doors and build upon it all their lives. I hope that association will help them keep society and all civilization in perspective with the world as a whole, and that they will always be concerned for the natural world and want to help take care of it.

But even if they never go camping a day in their lives once they've grown up and left our home, I think they've gained a lot already from the experience the wilderness has allowed them. They've learned a lot about the world and its creatures. They've had a great deal of time and attention from their father and me, an amount of time we probably would not have found it possible to give if we stayed at home, with all its endless work and responsibilities. And they've gained a lot of confidence in their own abilities by conquering some of the tasks they've been called on to perform in the wilderness. Once, when my older daughter was unhappy because she couldn't match the ability of some of her older friends in a game of baseball, I reminded her of all the things she could do well. She can ski, hike a long distance, paddle a canoe, and swim. Some of her older playmates have never even tried many of these activities. She felt better, and I had found another way in which wilderness camping enriched her life.

Why do I think you should try wilderness camping? Because it just may be as refreshing for you and your family as it is for us. Because you may find it an enjoyable vacation or even an enjoyable way of live. Because it can add so much to your life, to your child's life, and to your life together. The only way you'll know it can really be this great is to try it. So, why not give it a try?

12. "IN WILDERNESS ..."

The preservation of man and woman and child is indeed related to the preservation of the wilderness. The wilderness is a retreat from the sometimes overwhelming pressures of civilization. For so many of us it is an irreplaceable source of renewal, as well as an area where our fitness and resources are bettered because of its challenges and rewards.

The wilderness is vulnerable. It is not only up to us to help to preserve the wilderness, but up to our children, our grandchildren, and each succeeding generation. How can we best prepare our own children to meet the challenge of preserving our wilderness areas? One way we can help is to teach our children early to love the wilderness and to respect its needs and the delicate balance of our relationship with it. A visit to Niagara Falls disappoints me because I don't need the colored lights to enhance its beauty. I'd find it more beautiful, more impressive, illuminated by sunshine or moonlight. Who is more apt to protect our wild areas from desecration? Rather than the tourist who stops briefly to admire beauty from a car window, it is the person who has experienced the wilderness intimately and has grown to know and respect her who will fight for her survival.

Perhaps the best way to prepare our children and yours to protect the wild areas, is by introducing them to the wilderness at an early age. We can encourage them through our examples to love and respect the wilderness. By close association, I hope my children will develop an appreciation so great that they will fight for the preservation of the wilderness which, as Thoreau put it a century ago, is directly related to our own preservation.

APPENDIX I. Related Books and Periodicals

There is a vast library of literature dealing with the out-of-doors. I know because my house is cluttered with books on related subjects, and my collection represents only a sampling of those books available. Why not clutter up your house? The more extensive your knowledge of the area of the wilderness you explore, the more complete your experience will be. And, if you chose only a seasonal outdoor sport, such as bicycling or ski-touring, then your library will give you some vicarious enjoyment during the off months.

Who knows? Maybe if you choose a book on a new sport or technique, you may find yourself a new wilderness hobby. Lastly, no one can acquire too much knowledge in such important fields as first aid and orienteering. So I offer you a sampling of book and magazine titles to enrich your wilderness experiences, and to get you through that occasional long Sunday afternoon when you find yourself stuck at home.

Periodicals

1. *Backpacker;* E. D. Sheffe, ed; Ziff-Davis Publishing Co., 1 Park Ave., New York, N.Y. 10016.
2. *Better Camping and Hiking;* Kirk Landers, ed.; Woodall Publishing Co., 500 Hyacinth Place, Highland Park, IL 60035.
3. *Bicycling!;* James C. McCullagh, ed.; Rodeo Press, Emmaus Pennsylvania.
4. *Boys' Life;* Robert Hood, ed.; Boy Scouts of America, Dallas, Texas.
5. *Canoe;* American Canoe Association. The Web Company, 1999 Shepard Road, St. Paul, Minnesota.
6. *Nordic Skiing;* Nordic Skiing, Inc., Barbara Bruster, ed., Box 106, West Brattleboro, VT.
7. *Outside;* John Rasmus, Managing editor; 3401 W. Division Street, Chicago, IL.
8. *Ranger Rick;* Rickey Dahne, ed. National Wildlife Federation, Washington, D.C.
9. *River World;* World Publications, Mountain View, California 94040
10. *Ski Magazine's Guide to Cross-Country Skiing;* John Fry, ed.; Times Mirror Magazines, Inc.; 380 Madison Ave., New York, NY 10017.
11. *Skier's World;* World Publications, Mountain View, California 94040.

Books

1. *The Sierra Club Wilderness Handbook* David Brower, ed., Ballantine Books, New York, NY.
2. *Introduction to Backpacking,* Robert Colwell, Stackpole Books, Harrisburg, PA 17105.
3. *The New Complete Walker,* Colin Fletcher, Alfred A. Knopf Publishing, New York.
4. *Be Expert with Map and Compass,* Bjorn Knellstrom, American Orienteering Service, LaPorte, IN 46350.
5. *The Wilderness Handbook,* Paul Petzoldt, Alfred A. Knopf Publishing, New York.
6. *Creative Fitness for Baby and Child,* Suzy Prudden, Prentice-Hall, New York.
7. *Movin' Out, Equipment and Technique for Hikers,* Harry Roberts, Stone Wall Press, Washington, D.C.
8. *Backpacking with Babies and Small Children,* Goldie Silverman, Signpost Publications, Lynwood, WA.
9. *Backpacking with Small Children,* Jane and Ann Stout, Funk and Wagnalls, New York.
10. *Free for the Eating, More Free for the Eating Wild Foods, Wilderness Cookery, Living Off the Country* (four books); Bradford Angier, Stackpole Books, Harrisburg, PA 17105.
11. *Being Your Own Wilderness Doctor,* Kodet and Angier, Stackpole Books, Harrisburg, PA 17105.
12. *The Cross-Country Ski Book,* John Caldwell, Stephen Greene Press, Brattleboro, VT.
13. *Cross-Country Skiing;* Ned Gillette, The Mountaineers, Seattle, WA.
14. *Movin' On, Equipment and Technique for Winter Hikers,* Harry Roberts, Stone Wall Press, Washington, D.C. 20007.
15. *Canoeing,* American Red Cross.
16. *The Canoe Camper's Handbook,* Ray Bearse, Winchester Press, New York, NY 10022.
17. *The Complete Wilderness Paddler,* James West Davidson and John Rugge, Afred A. Knopf, New York, NY.
18. *Basic River Canoeing,* Robert McNair, American Camping Association, Martinsville, IN 46151.

19. *Anybody's Bike Book,* Tom Cuthbertson, Ten Speed Press, Berkeley, CA 94704.
20. *Bike Tripping,* Tom Cuthbertson, Ten Speed Press, Berkeley, CA 94704.
21. *Two Wheel Travel: Bicycle Camping and Touring,* Peter Tobey, ed; Dell Publishing Co., New York, NY 10017.
22. *Derailleur Bicycle Repair,* XYZ Information Corporation, Cayoga Park, CA 91303.
23. *DeLong's Guide to Bicycles and Bicycling,* Fred DeLong, Chilton Book Co., Radnor, PA.

APPENDIX II. Mail Order Supply Houses

These dealers supply all the equipment necessary to participate in the sports described in this book. While there are others, this is an assortment of dealers with whom I have had both experience and satisfaction.

1. Akers Ski, Andover, ME 04216
   Akers handles cross-country ski equipment, clothing and other ski-related accessories. They have a good line of children's equipment, and their service is unbelievably prompt. The catalog is free.
2. Early Winters, Ltd., 110 Prefontaine Place So., Seattle, WA 98104.
   Specializing in Gore-tex and fiberpile. No bargains, but truly top-flight items are featured by this company.
3. Eastern Mountain Sports, One Vose Farm Road, Peterborough, NH 03458.
   This store has eleven different branches all over the country and is a leader in all sorts of wilderness equipment. The catalog costs $1.00, but is a virtual encyclopedia of knowledge as well as a showplace of equipment.
4. Eddie Bauer, Dept. JBP, Fifth & Union, Seattle, WA 98124.
   Bauer's is one of the best known manufacturers of down clothing and other such gear for recreational use. The catalog is free.

5. Frostline, 452 Burbank, Broomfield, CO 80020.
Frostline provides free catalogs on request presenting their line of kits for making quality clothing, tents, sleeping bags, and packs suitable for wilderness camping.
6. Indiana Camp Supply, Inc., P.O. Box 344, Pittsboro, IN 46167.
An excellent source of trail foods and first-aid/medical supplies, as well as more standard types of gear.
7. L. L. Bean, Freeport, ME 04033.
Beans is almost a legend. There is a song about it, and they have even published their own "guide" to the outdoors. They have a complete line of merchandise for canoeing, camping, and ski touring. Free catalog.
8. Moor and Mountain, 63 Park St., Andover, MA 01810.
This free catalog is filled with equipment for family wilderness sports. (This is where I bought those economical children's rucksacks.)
9. Recreational Equipment, Inc., P.O. Box C-88127, Seattle, WA 98188.
A very complete catalog, full of camping clothing and equipment of all kinds, and at competitive prices.
10. The Ski Hut, 1615 University Ave., Berkeley, CA 94703.
For fifty cents you can acquire a catalog which includes many items for backpacking and other forms of wilderness camping, as well as skiing.

Photo Credits

Other STONE WALL PRESS Outdoor Books:

Backbacking for Trout, by Bill Cairns, introduction by "Lefty" Kreh. Written by the founder of the famous Orvis Fly Casting School, this practical book is for any fisherman—novice or expert—who wants to successfully fish the quiet streams, ponds, and lakes of the backwoods. Illustrated. $16.95 hardback.

The Natural World Cookbook, by Joe Freitus. A complete and comprehensive cookbook of wild, edible foods for the adventuresome gourmet. You will find hundreds of recipes for complete meals that can be prepared from abundant wild foods found across North America. Both plants and animals are included, along with beautiful line drawings for their easy identification by Salli Haberman. Illustrated. $25.00 hardback.

Movin' Out, Equipment and Technique for Hikers, by Harry Roberts. The editor of *Wilderness Camping* magazine has put together a practical, no nonsense book for backpacking. His solid advice on choosing the right equipment and how to use it make this book indispensible for the beginning or experienced backpacker. Illustrated. $7.95 paperback.

Movin' On, Equipment and Technique for Winter Hikers, by Harry Roberts. This companion volume takes a solid what-works approach to winter hiking and camping. "This is a *superb* book, even if you are just thinking about *maybe* going winter camping." Illustrated. $7.95 paperback.

Backwoods Ethics, by Guy and Laura Waterman. "... undeniably important. They argue that hikers and backpackers must protect natural resources and maintain the 'spirit of wildness' of our country's backwoods ... they describe a new code of backwoods ethics they feel is necessary to accommodate the increasing number of hikers in the wilds."—*Publishers Weekly.* Positive and up-beat, this book documents progress while appealing to a raised natural consciousness. Illustrations. $8.95, paperback.

If these titles are unavailable through your bookstore, please send us your check or money order for the price of the book, plus $2.00 postage and handling, along with your printed name, address and ZIP. Thank you!

STONE WALL PRESS, INC.
1241 30th Street, N.W., Washington, D.C. 20007